"This is a great book, filled with m.
person and work of Jesus. Ground.   ....
testimony), it helps us think through how and why we try to escape—and
what gospel change looks like."

Emma Scrivener, *author of A New Name and A New Day*

"This book is easy to read, and full of self-deprecating humour, with plenty of
practical examples of people like you and me. Reading a book on escaping
escapism is the easy bit, but Dave explores the wisdom contained in Scripture
and a relationship with God that truly helps us in our daily lives. This is a
hopeful and encouraging book."

Michael Harvey, *co-founder of Back to Church Sunday; author of
Unlocking the Growth*

"As someone who struggles with passivity in leadership, I needed this book.
Dave Griffith-Jones not only coins an important new term for our struggles—
for the disobedience that masks itself as risk-avoidance—but gives a gospel-
saturated, compassionate call to repent of our inaction and courageously live
out the life of Christ."

Daniel Darling, *Vice-President for Communications, Ethics & Religious
Liberty Commission of the Southern Baptist Convention*

"We're a distracted generation. And moralism is as useless a solution as it's
always been. Dave has served us with insight, stimulus and encouragement
from the Scriptures and church history, helping us not just to replace one
escapism with another, but to engage our wavering, hungering hearts.
Recommended—an excellent book."

Ben Virgo, *Director of Christian Heritage London*

Foreword by
RICO TICE

Escaping
escapism

DAVE GRIFFITH-JONES

For Helen,
living proof that Proverbs 18 v 22 is true

Escaping Escapism *Stop putting things off. Start taking things on.*
© Dave Griffith-Jones/The Good Book Company, 2018.

Published by
The Good Book Company
Tel (UK): 0333 123 0880
International: +44 (0) 208 942 0880
Email: info@thegoodbook.co.uk

Websites:
North America: www.thegoodbook.com
UK: www.thegoodbook.co.uk
Australia: www.thegoodbook.com.au
New Zealand: www.thegoodbook.co.nz

ISBN: 9781784981808 | Printed in the UK

Cover design by ninefootone creative

Contents

Foreword
By Rico Tice

It was a Sunday night at All Souls Langham Place in London, the church at which I serve. It was 20th November 1994, and Alec Motyer, the theologian and preacher from Ireland, was speaking on the 500th anniversary of William Tyndale, the man who translated the Bible into English so that a plough boy might read God's word, and who was martyred for his work.

I remember that Sunday night because of one question Alec Motyer asked, which seared itself onto my heart. As he lamented the absence of a reformation in the southern part of Ireland, he wondered why his homeland never had one. Why did the ploughboy in Wicklow not get a Bible in his own language? It was because, he thundered, there was no Irish Tyndale.

And, he said, perhaps God had called such a man to do that work—*and he turned away.*

I was cut to the heart. Alec Motyer, of course, was talking about the subject of this book: the sin of omission. Not so much the sins I have done, but the things that, in my laziness and self-centredness, I have left undone. And it is this point, so profoundly explored and illustrated in this book that you are holding right now, that causes me to make a confession about my confession, whether when leading public worship or in personal prayer.

It's this: I hardly ever touch on what I fail to do.

I have been a Christian for over 30 years now, but I've been challenged by this book all over again, just as I was back in 1994 in that sermon and by that question. I've been struck by what I should do but don't—what I turn away from. And that's a good thing, because those sins of omission are what prevent me from doing and being all that God calls me to do and be, and what those around me need me to do and be.

What makes this book compelling is that it touches on a profound danger for us. We are so very good at seeing the foolishness of the sins others commit by what they do. So on the whole we know that adultery destroys families, and alcohol destroys livers, and tempers destroy relationships. We are far less good at seeing the foolishness of the sins we commit by what we do not do. The great danger for committed Christians is to avoid those sins of commission, and feel good about doing so, even as we commit the great sin of omission in simply never serving and living for Jesus wholeheartedly.

Francis Schaeffer, the Christian apologist and founder of L'Abri, said in his book *How Should We Then Live?* (first published in 1976) that the temptation for Christians during the following 60 years would be personal peace and affluence. He was not wrong. To put it another way, our greatest danger is that we avoid doing what Paul called Timothy (and through him the Spirit calls us) to do: to suffer for the gospel, to live as a soldier, an athlete, a farmer (2 Timothy 2 v 3-7). In other words, to take on the hard things that the Lord calls us to do, and say, and be, in order to love the gospel and love people.

So, as you read this book, hold onto your seat, because the way in which we have let ourselves fall into the sin of omission is brutally revealed, even as the way of knowing Christ better is wonderfully shown to be what we truly need. After all, surely the most helpful books are not the ones that are easiest to read, but those that reveal to us what sin, the world and the devil have been doing in our lives without us even noticing. This book will do that for you, and then it will show you what a renewed vision of Christ would do in those areas of our lives where we've been failing, so that you might become more and more like him.

The call of the gospel is the call to a hard life, rather than a comfortable one—the life that, for example, Dave took his family into when he chose to pastor in the inner city of Liverpool. It's a life of hard choices made for the sake of the gospel. It's not a life of ease or escapism.

So this book is a profoundly important contribution to our evangelical Christian culture. It is a brilliant antidote to the sins of omission that are such a danger and so hard to spot, and it is a wonderful portrait of the Lord Jesus as our refuge, shepherd, light, portion, rock, strength and salvation. It will lead you away from self-confidence, and inspire you to have the Christ-confidence which alone will enable you to stop escaping and start loving and truly living, until the glorious day when we see the Lord Jesus face to face.

Rico Tice,
Senior Minister at All Souls Langham Place, London
Founder of Christianity Explored Ministries

1. The best things we do

The best things we do are usually the hardest.

Like climbing mountains. I love climbing mountains—especially Scottish mountains. Yet it's always a battle to put my boots on and set out. My legs ache, the weather looks unpleasant (Scottish mountain weather has its own type of "forbidding grey") and I know the midges will be fierce (if you haven't experienced Scottish midges, think vicious squadrons of miniature airborne piranhas).

It's less risky and more comfortable to stay on the sofa watching daytime TV. It's easier not to bother.

But by packing my rucksack and heading out and climbing hard, I've seen the sun setting over the Western Isles, come face to face with a golden eagle, and ascended through the clouds to sun-drenched mountaintop worlds. The path is steep but the view from the top is worth it.

The best things we do are usually the hardest.

Like the day I proposed to Helen. It was terrifying. (Just to be clear, it's not Helen that's terrifying; just the thought that she might say no). We were at a beautiful waterfall, the moment was perfect... but my tongue and my stomach had both tied themselves into Gordian knots. The nerves made me so quiet that Helen thought I was in a bad mood with her, so she got in a bad mood with me. By the time I finally blurted out the question, she was cold, hungry and thoroughly fed up. I considered putting it off to another day. But eventually out came the words, she said yes, and now the girl of my dreams has been my wife for twelve years.

The best things we do are usually the hardest.

Then there's my job. Five years ago our family moved to Toxteth, Liverpool—renowned as one of the most deprived inner-city communities in England—and I started working at a church there. In some difficult moments it did live down to its reputation—not being able to take the kids to the playground because someone was selling crack on the swings, the gang of youths who aimed a firework at my one-year-old daughter, the odd shooting, the eye-watering car insurance premiums. But mostly it was brilliant. We've met some wonderful people, enjoyed the great Liverpool parks and museums and docks and humour, and seen Jesus at work in and through the people in our church. There is nowhere else we'd rather have been.

What's really worth it

Leaving home and making new friends, speaking in public for the first time, being a dad, learning to pray, opening my home and cooking a meal for people, telling friends about Jesus—the things I most dreaded doing have been the things I most delighted in doing. Even when I've failed, I've been glad that I gave it a go.

It's probably been the same for you: learning a language, training for a triathlon, starting a new business... the most daunting tasks are also the most rewarding. Whether it's committing to a relationship or confronting a problem that you've avoided for too long, the most fulfilling experiences come from tackling the most frightening challenges. It's the only way to be free from selfishness and boredom. As the spy, inventor, fighter pilot and children's author Roald Dahl said, "Most of the really exciting things we do in our lives scare us to death; they wouldn't be exciting if they didn't".

Almost anything that is worth doing is a struggle. Almost anything that benefits other people is tough to do. Almost anything that makes a difference in this world is hard to see through to the end.

Which is why, we'll often do almost anything to escape doing it.

I guess you've picked up this book because you want to love difficult people, tackle difficult challenges and keep moving forwards through difficult times. You want to get on with doing hard things, fix what needs fixing and change what needs changing. But you know that those things don't come naturally. You know they require lots of commitment, courage and integrity. You'd need to stop taking the easy way out, ducking awkward conversations, and putting off anything inconvenient until tomorrow. You'd have to start rising to the challenges of life, and being resilient when relationships and jobs are demanding.

I would love to be this kind of person—wouldn't you? Wouldn't it be good to be someone who isn't put off by the size or scale or cost of a worthwhile task? Wouldn't it be great to be fearless, to embrace responsibility, and to live with integrity? Wouldn't you love to see a diet or exercise plan through to the finish, just for once?

That's the person I want to be. That's the person I've sometimes been (when the weather forecast has been good).

But often it's not the person I choose to be. I find myself putting off unpleasant tasks. I'm addicted to live text commentaries of sporting events when I should be talking to my children. I feel sick at the thought of giving an honest answer to a personal question. I follow the advice of that renowned life coach, Homer Simpson:

"If something's hard to do, then it's not worth doing."

This book started out as a quest to discover why I'm not the strong and courageous person I want to be (and which the people I love need me to be), and how I could become that person. The good news is I've found the answers—they're in the Bible. The Bible has shown me why I act this way. It's told me how I can be changed and made committed and fearless. And it's shown me the one person in history who has lived the life we all long to live—Jesus.

Jesus always loved difficult people. He compassionately taught and fed the crowds when they interrupted his plans. He courageously spoke the truth to groups who had the power to kill him. He persevered with friends who misunderstood him, criticised him and deserted him. He looked out for others when his life was at his hardest.

Jesus always tackled difficult challenges. He made unpopular decisions. He did what God wanted even when his own family disapproved. He broke social conventions around women, immigrants and lepers. He challenged human injustice and demonic evil. He didn't shy away from the glare of publicity or the gloom of obscurity.

Jesus always persevered through difficult times. He resolutely walked towards a city where he knew that he must suffer and die. He was resilient when falsely accused, beaten, spat on, mocked, stripped naked and nailed to a cross. He endured the pain of being separated from his Father out of love for undeserving people like us. He took on the hardest path known to man, and reached its end. He never, ever ducked out.

The Bible doesn't just show us that this is what Jesus is like. It also shows us how we can become like him. How we can live with Jesus' courage, integrity and love. How you can.

Because the Bible promises that God can give us an undivided heart.

With an undivided heart...

... an unreliable young man can learn to commit—to a job, a church, a friend, a wife, a child.

... an employee who can't start work without checking her notifications can become the treasured colleague who attempts the hardest jobs first.

... a self-conscious introvert who is anxious about meeting new people can begin to look out for and welcome the outsider.

... a student who copies work off the internet can gain the integrity to do their own work.

... a girl who is scared to aim high and end up looking stupid can give things a go without being afraid of failure.

... a dad who hides in the shed because he feels out of his depth forming relationships can be the engaged, confident and vulnerable husband and father his family need.

The very best things we do are usually the very hardest. And an undivided heart is the spring from which a fearless life that does those things flows. It's the key to loving difficult people, tackling difficult challenges and persevering through difficult times. It's the secret to being strong and courageous.

My heart's desire for myself in the last few years has been for God to give me an undivided heart. My heart's desire for this book is that God will use it to do the same for you. Here's the God-given prayer that I've prayed for myself almost every day for the last few years, and that I'd encourage you to make your own as you read this book:

"Teach me your way, LORD,
    that I may rely on your faithfulness;
give me an undivided heart,
    that I may fear your name." (Psalm 86 v 11)

It's time to stop escaping and start advancing.

2. A divided heart

Harry Houdini is renowned as the greatest escapologist. His signature escape was the "Chinese Water Torture Cell". Enclosed in a cage with his hands cuffed and his feet locked in stocks, he took a deep breath and was lowered upside down into a huge tank of water. A curtain concealed him from his paying audience, while an orchestra played "Asleep in the Deep". An axe was kept ready to break the tank in case of emergency. But after two minutes of tension, Houdini always appeared around the curtain, unshackled and free.

Though no one pays to watch me, I too have turned escape into an art form. I've spent 37 years learning to avoid difficult people, put off difficult challenges and give up in difficult times.

A portrait of the escape artist as a young man

I was that kid who suddenly decides to stop playing tag when they're about to be caught. I was the schoolboy who just happened to feel sick on the day when there was a German test. I would do the simple homework due in next week instead of the difficult homework due in tomorrow. I would write a revision timetable to delay doing any revision. When I fell out with a teacher, I skipped his lessons to avoid the awkwardness of saying sorry. When I broke something at home, I would carefully replace it to make the next person who touched it think they had done it. (That rarely worked.)

I haven't grown out of it. I'm a river flowing down the path of least resistance. Why talk about things that matter when I can stick to banter and jokes? Why say sorry when I can avoid the person I've hurt or let down until they've forgotten about it? It's less painful to cover up mistakes than to admit them. It's less effort to surf the web on my phone than to give my children proper attention. I do what is easy instead of what is right.

Or, I don't do anything at all. My favourite tactic for escaping difficult jobs is to write a to-do list at the start of each week to delay doing any of the jobs on it. At the end of the week the items still on that list will be the important jobs I just don't want to do. Some have been there for so long they were written with a quill. Where does the time go? It might have something to do with how many times each day I have to check my email, Twitter, news websites, Facebook, blogs, YouTube, and fantasy football team. And then I check Twitter and the news websites again, just in case something has happened in the last ten minutes.

I try to turn escapism to my advantage. I motivate myself to start one task by threatening myself with the far more difficult work I ought to be doing. I mess around with the kids when I don't want to work, and I work when the kids mess me around. If I don't want to do either, then there's always Netflix.

Perhaps my greatest escapism triumph is the dentist. I last visited a dentist in 1997. At first I thought it was a waste of time and money. Then I reasoned that I would go when my

18

teeth hurt. Now my teeth hurt and I'm too scared to go. I'd rather not know how rotten they are, and I don't want the pain of treatment. I'm dooming myself to worse pain in the future, but that's the way with escapism.

You may not have quite such a bad case of it as I do, but I am guessing that there are symptoms of escapism in your life too. Because I know that escapism is a pretty popular pastime—even the heavyweight boxing champion Anthony Joshua recently admitted that his training suffered because he spent too much time playing FIFA.

There are many ways you might be avoiding difficult things. You can tell the easy lie instead of the hard truth; you can turn to soft drugs instead of facing up to hard problems. You might be the man in his thirties still living with his mum and playing Xbox for hours; or the woman in her forties reading erotic fiction rather than improving her real-world relationships; or the retired couple going on a three-month cruise when their children are desperate for help with childcare. You might be the teenager cheating in exams because for you, your value depends on your results; you might be the teacher letting her cheat because your value depends on her results too. You might be the lazy boy nagging his mum to do his homework for him; you might be his mum, giving in because that's easier than having an argument.

What difficult things are you avoiding, right now? Being honest about your struggles, rescuing a failing marriage, or sorting out your debts? Are you saying no to a suitable relationship because you're scared of commitment; or saying yes to an unsuitable or immoral relationship because you're scared of singleness? Are you staying late at work to escape problems at home; or staying home all day to escape work? Are you one of the thousands of husbands who stay at home on Sundays to get away from thinking about God? Are you one of the many wives who go to church to get away from home and husband? After church, do you chat to others to avoid serving in some way that you don't find very attractive; or do you get on with serving so that you don't have to chat to others?

We are very resourceful when it comes to finding ways to escape doing the right thing, the best thing, the greatest thing. Some of us even escape by reading books on escapism. Some of us do it by writing them.

Why does it even matter though?

Three reasons...

First, because *we hate our escapism*. Escapism means that we miss out on so much of what makes life worth living: deep relationships with friends and family, and the satisfaction of having achieved and finished something—a DIY project or a degree or a dress you've made. Escapists never stand on the summit of a mountain they've climbed (literally or metaphorically). Escapists never become the people they could be.

Second, because *the people around us hate our escapism*. Our escapism means that the people we love miss out on so much of what makes life worth living too. Our friends and family miss out on deep relationships with us. They are let down every time we choose what is easy for us instead of what is best for them. When someone asks for volunteers and we look at the floor because we want to binge-watch the latest box set; when we avoid the neighbour whose husband has just died because we're worried we wouldn't know what to say; when we cancel coffee with an old friend because we left a piece of work until the day before the deadline—it's not just you whose life is that much worse. When the going gets tough, the escapist pulls a sickie and leaves everyone else to clear up the mess.

So much good is left undone because we aren't strong and courageous. Truth doesn't get told, work doesn't get finished, spouses don't get cherished, children don't get parented, injustice doesn't get challenged, inventions don't get made, art doesn't get created, churches don't get planted, sinners don't get told the good news, neighbours don't get loved, Jesus doesn't get honoured.

Third, because *God hates our escapism*. Escapism is serious because it offends the God who made us and who loves us. Here's the thing: escapism isn't just a shame; it's a sin. Sins come in two shades. A sin of commission is doing something bad that God tells us *not* to do. A sin of omission is not doing something good that God tells us *to* do. Escapist sins tend to be sins of omission. Escapists tend not to commit murder or rob banks (that would require courage), but escapists also don't confront the office bully or serve the poor.

The church tends to focus on the first set of sins—sins of commission. Think of the sermons you've heard, the books you've read, the warnings other Christians have given you or you've given others, and the sins your own conscience is sensitive about. I'm almost certain they focus on avoiding sins of commission, rather than avoiding sins of omission.

So when I became a Christian aged 19, the first sins that I fought were sins of commission—getting drunk, telling lewd jokes, insulting people, lust. But for years I was never that bothered about my sins of omission. I kept on being lazy, not saying sorry, only talking to people I found interesting. And I thought that I was living a reasonably godly life, stopping doing the things God told me not to.

Yet Jesus says that the worst sin in the world is a sin not of commission, but of omission. When someone asked Jesus what God's most important command was, he said this:

> "The most important one ... is this: 'Hear, O Israel: the Lord our God, the Lord is one. Love the Lord your God with all your heart and with all your soul and with all your mind and with all your strength.' The second is this: 'Love your neighbour as yourself.' There is no commandment greater than these." (Mark 12 v 29-31)

This, says Jesus, is what God made you for. But escapism is a failure to love God and to love people. Our most important priority in life is the very activity that escapism keeps us from doing. Escapists miss out on the true purpose of life (no wonder they find life such a boring and unsatisfying existence).

But stopping there would be to miss the point of what Jesus is saying. The evil of escapism isn't how it makes me feel; it's how it makes God feel. Even when I'm not disturbed by my escapism, God is. Even when I'm OK with it, God is offended by it.

So don't just read this book because you hate escapism; read this book because God hates escapism. Fight escapism, because it really is the worst sin in the world.

Where does it come from?

Fear is the root of all escapism.

Fear is living in awe of someone or something. It's a type of faith—it's believing that something has power over our future and our happiness. This thing seems so big or so beautiful to us that it becomes all-important—we can't risk losing it. If

I think I can't be happy if I'm not comfortable, I live in awe of my comfort and will never do anything that risks making my life less pleasant. If I'm in awe of my friend or partner or parent, I'll always seek to please them and will avoid doing anything that risks upsetting them.

Inside Out is a Pixar movie based inside an 11-year-old girl, Riley, and starring her five dominant emotions: Joy, Sadness, Anger, Disgust and Fear. Fear gives up when things get difficult:

> "Quitting; that's what I'm doing. Sure, it's the coward's way out—but this coward's going to survive."

Fear is an escapist. And we don't just see this in pop psychology—you can see the effect of fear in your own life. Do you ever do easy tasks before important ones because you fear failure or hard work? Do you avoid going to the doctor or admitting that you struggle with depression or doubts because you're afraid other people will think you're weak? Do you choose to have low aspirations and not try new things because you're anxious you will fail if you set your sights any higher? Are you scared of moving out, or moving on, because you're fearful of not being in control? Inside every escapist is a heart beating to the rhythm of fear.

We've already looked at the most important command in the Bible. Now let's look at the most repeated command in the Bible. It's not "love one another" or "pray more" or "listen when your dad is talking to you and do what he says" (unfortunately). It's this:

> "Do not be afraid."

So far I've found that command a staggering 144 times in the Bible—and there are probably some more I haven't spotted.

Do not be afraid. Why does God say this so often in the Bible? Because fear is the enemy of love. The most repeated command shows us why we don't keep the most important command. Fear stops me loving God, because I'm scared that I'll miss out on something better. Fear stops me loving other people, because I'm anxious that there will be no one left to love me.

The Bible is full of stories of people engaging in selfish, escapist behaviour. Each time, the root cause is fear. Here's a small sample:

- Abraham has to migrate to Egypt briefly to escape a famine. He's worried, because his wife, Sarah, has a model's good looks. Pharaoh might decide he wants her for himself. So Abraham tells Sarah to lie and pretend she's his sister, and then pimps his wife to the king because, even though she'll be sexually assaulted, that way he'll be spared. Why does he lie? Because he's afraid (Genesis 12 v 10-20).

- When King David is on the run from Saul, he heads for a Philistine city called Gath. This is a bit of a problem, because David has made a career out of fighting and killing Philistines (starting with the fearsome Goliath). So the once-brave warrior feigns madness to survive, scratching on doors and dribbling down his hipster beard. Why? Because he's afraid (1 Samuel 21 v 10-15).

- On the night that Jesus is arrested, all of his friends desert him and go into hiding in case they're taken with him. One of them has "gone commando", wearing nothing under his tunic. When a soldier grabs it, he slips it off and endures the shame of streaking stark naked through the streets of

Jerusalem to get away. Why? Because he's afraid (Mark 14 v 50-52).

David summed up how he felt in a song. Abraham and the unknown not-so-great follower of Jesus could have written these words too:

"My heart is in anguish within me;
   the terrors of death have fallen on me.
Fear and trembling have beset me;
   horror has overwhelmed me.
I said, 'Oh, that I had the wings of a dove!
   I would fly away and be at rest.
I would flee far away
   and stay in the desert.'" (Psalm 55 v 4-7)

Escapism comes from a heart beating to the rhythm of fear. It is, in fact, a form of heart disease, because it comes from having a divided heart.

When the Bible talks about "the heart", it means the control centre of a human—the real you that lies behind all your attitudes, actions and inactions. With your heart, you think and trust and believe; and with your heart, you desire and love and fear and worship.

The Bible says the whole of your lifestyle flows from your heart in the same way the whole of a river flows from a spring (Proverbs 4 v 23). Jesus says you can recognise the health of someone's heart by their words and actions in just the same way you can recognise the health of a tree by its fruit (Luke 6 v 43-45). A person with a greedy heart is recognised by their greedy actions; a person with an honest heart is recognised by their honest words; and a person with an escapist heart is recognised by the number of unopened bills lying by their front door. More seriously, the escapist heart is recognised by the fruit of boredom, addiction, distraction, laziness, weakness, fickleness, shallowness, self-pity and self-despair.

This is strong stuff. It's the sort of diagnosis a doctor only tells you when you're sitting down. Jesus is saying that I'm not a strong and courageous person who occasionally does weak and cowardly things. I do escapist things because I've got an escapist heart. I fail to love God and love others because I've got a divided heart. And if my heart's the problem, then any cure will need to operate at the level of my heart. It's going to require major surgery.

God created us to believe and love and fear one thing: himself. That's the logic of the most important command: "The Lord is one"—he's unique, he's the only God of the whole cosmos, the only one worthy of our delight and worship—so "love the Lord your God with all your heart". Fearing God alone is what alone liberates our hearts, because he alone really is the key to our future and our happiness.

But my escapist heart is torn by various fears. It's a divided heart. It doesn't trust and love and fear our one Creator, but instead trusts and loves and fears various created things. Like a cheating husband, my heart has other gods on the side as I worship a pantheon of non-gods. Every time I back away from a difficult conversation, and every time I back out of doing something hard, and every time I duck out of doing what's loving toward God and those he's placed around me, it's because I'm living in awe of a fake god instead of the real God.

A divided heart is a broken heart. This is what an escapist's broken heart can look like:

The heart diagram contains the following phrases:

- THE INTERNET IS MY REFUGE
- "NOT YET" IS MY ROCK
- NOT FAILING IS MY SALVATION
- ALCOHOL IS MY STRENGTH
- MY HOUSE IS MY SHEPHERD
- COMFORT IS MY PORTION
- FAMILY IS MY LIGHT

- Kayleigh feels nervous at a gathering where she doesn't know anyone, so she checks Facebook on her phone. The internet is her refuge.
- Mo is embarrassed that he lost his temper with someone at church, so he's staying at home and isn't answering the doorbell or the phone. His house is his shepherd.
- Tracy is struggling with her debts because she feels like she can't say no to her children's demands for toys and gadgets and outings. Her family are her light.
- Jeff keeps telling his wife he'll do those jobs around the house, but when he gets home in the evening he just wants to watch the football with a takeaway on his lap. His comfort is his portion.

- Meesha knows that she ought to see a bereavement counsellor after her mum died last year, but she's scared of bringing the pain back to the surface so she's putting it off. "Not yet" is her rock.
- Jason is overwhelmed by his problems and can't face the world without a drink inside him. Alcohol is his strength.
- Evie is very capable at her job and at relationships, but she keeps away from anything new or challenging, because deep down she needs to feel good about herself. Not failing is her salvation.

Evie is a good example of someone who looks hard-working because she is so in one area of life, but who is also anxious and uncommitted in another. The problem is that she is working hard out of a wrongly-placed fear. She is, in reality, working hard to escape. So is the teenager who practises for hours to become great on the guitar, but also plays truant from school because guitar-playing is his refuge. So is the woman who started up her own business, but is unable to make the first move to patch things up with the sister she isn't speaking to because business success is her strength. So is the athlete who is utterly dedicated to months of marathon training, but keeps letting down the depressed friend he has promised to visit because sport is his portion.

The jostling of "gods" in our divided hearts explain why Christians struggle with escapism. I've been trusting in Jesus' death to win me forgiveness and give me eternal life for 18 years, but I still fail to make him my refuge and so I procrastinate. I still don't tell my friends about him, because they are my light and I can't bear the thought of offending them. I need Jesus to be my everything, not just my eternity.

As we finish this chapter, it's time to undertake some difficult self-diagnosis. Pause for a moment to examine your heart. Try thinking and praying about these questions:

1. Are you an escapist? What are your regular sins of omission? Look for the symptoms of a broken heart in your life—difficult people whom you avoid, difficult tasks that you put off, and times when you've given up in difficult situations.

2. Can you identify what you fear when you hit the escape button? Try to name whom you are scared of upsetting, or what you are worried about losing. What are you living in awe of?

3. What escapes do you run to? What refuge do you hide in? What do you rely on to give you strength? What portion do you look to for solace when things go wrong?

This isn't easy for us. The truth about us is not as positive as we'd like it to be. But the great news is that Jesus promised:

> "It is not the healthy who need a doctor, but those who are ill. I have not come to call the righteous, but sinners to repentance." (Luke 5 v 31-32)

I've got a heart problem. So have you. But Jesus came to mend our broken hearts. The doctor will see us now...

3. How can you mend a broken heart?

Imagine a couple who are looking to buy and set up their first home together.

There are two stages.

In stage one, they purchase the house and move in. They put in an offer, exchange contracts, arrange the mortgage and pay the deposit. They get the keys and start living in the house.

In stage two, they do up the house to turn it into the home they desire. They replace the curtains and bring in their own furniture. They tear up the carpet because wooden floors are in fashion. A couple of years later, they put in a new kitchen. The year after that, they convert the attic into some office space for a new family business. Two years after that, one of the bedrooms needs redecorating as a nursery for a baby boy.

An escapist heart is like a rundown old home in need of some serious restoration work. The good news is that Jesus promises to mend our divided hearts—to restore these rickety tumbledown ruins and transform them into beautiful palaces.

This happens in the same two stages: first Jesus purchases us and moves in (this happens in a moment); then he sets to work redecorating and turning our hearts into the home he desires (this takes a lifetime). Wonderfully, his death on the cross has bought everything necessary for both the purchase and the renovation.

God moves in

The worst thing about being an escapist (or any other type of sinner) isn't that we miss out on a better life (though we do), but that we miss out on the presence of God. We don't just lose opportunities and friends; we lose God himself. Rather than enjoying God's infinite love for us, our hearts let squatters in—false gods and fears that divide our hearts by taking a room each, and then mess up our hearts by trashing the place.

This is how the apostle Paul describes it:

"Remember that at that time you were separate from Christ, excluded from citizenship in Israel and foreigners to the covenants of the promise, without hope and without God in the world..." (Ephesians 2 v 12)

That's our situation before we know Jesus: separated from Christ, the source of true wisdom and love; without any hope of being cured and set free; with no access to the God who gives us joy and purpose; hope-less and God-less.

That's not where the story ends, though:

"But now in Christ Jesus you who once were far away have been brought near by the blood of Christ."

(Ephesians 2 v 13)

"But now" is always a phrase in the Bible that signals good news. Any and every Christian was a deserted ruin, far away from

God; but now every Christian is a treasured home, brought near to God by the blood of Christ, shed as he died on the cross.

Jesus is the only person who always lived with an undivided heart. He always loved God alone and feared God alone. He never ducked out or backed out of doing what was right and loving. And because he loved us, he did not back down even from taking the punishment that our divided, false-god-squat hearts deserve. On the cross, Jesus was separated from God so that we could be reunited with God. He was evicted so that we could come home. His hope was cut off so that we could be given hope. He endured God's absence so that we could enjoy God's presence. His blood cleanses us in God's sight so that God can be pleased to dwell in us again.

Here's the result:

> "Consequently, you are no longer foreigners and strangers, but fellow citizens with God's people and also members of his household, built on the foundation of the apostles and prophets, with Christ Jesus himself as the chief cornerstone. In him the whole building is joined together and rises to become a holy temple in the Lord. And in him you too are being built together to become a dwelling in which God lives by his Spirit."
>
> (Ephesians 2 v 19-22)

If you are a Christian, you are no longer a foreigner but a citizen; no longer a stranger but a member of God's family; no longer a rat-infested ruin but now a holy temple that God delights to live in by his Spirit. Once we were broken, but now we're being rebuilt.

That passage is talking about God living in us as a church together, but the same is true personally for every individual who trusts in Jesus:

"Do you not know that your bodies are temples of the Holy Spirit, who is in you, whom you have received from God? You are not your own; you were bought at a price. Therefore honour God with your bodies."

(1 Corinthians 6 v 19-20)

When Jesus died on the cross, he purchased us. He paid the price to ransom us so that we now belong to him. He overthrew the squatters in our hearts and has evicted them. He is our new owner. He has the keys. And because we are his, he has moved in—by his Holy Spirit he has taken up residence in our hearts.

Because of the Son of God's death for us, we can enjoy God's presence moment by moment, day by day, through his Spirit. Most of this book will be focused on how God works to free us from our escapism, but don't miss this, because it all starts here. The best gift God gives us isn't a better life; it's himself.

God starts mending

There's still the second stage once God has moved in, though—when God's Spirit starts doing the place up. Room by room, the work of rebuilding and redecoration begins in our hearts, so that we become the home that Jesus desires. The Spirit is working in our hearts to restore them so that we love God alone and fear God alone. One of the greatest prayers we can pray for ourselves and for other Christians is that the Spirit would do this renovation work:

"I pray that out of his glorious riches [the Father] may strengthen you with power through his Spirit in your inner being, so that Christ may dwell in your hearts through faith. And I pray that you, being rooted and

established in love, may have power, together with all
the Lord's holy people, to grasp how wide and long and
high and deep is the love of Christ, and to know this
love that surpasses knowledge—that you may be filled
to the measure of all the fullness of God."

(Ephesians 3 v 16-19)

Like the young couple redecorating their first home, Jesus
still has work to do. As we grasp how much Christ loves us,
his Spirit fills us with all God's fullness. Increasingly, every
room is filled with the presence and character of Jesus, who
has always loved and feared God with an undivided heart.

To see what this means and how it happens, let's go back to
two passages in the Old Testament that looked forward to the
day when our divided hearts could be restored.

A promise for broken hearts

God's Old Testament people, Israel, were sent away from God's
presence and into exile because they had divided hearts—they
worshipped other gods and feared the nations around them
instead of being in awe of God alone. Through his prophet
Jeremiah, God made one of my favourite promises in the Old
Testament. This promise looked forward to the day when God
would make a new covenant with his people—which he has
done through Jesus dying and rising again (a covenant is a
binding promise). So this is a promise for every person—
including every escapist—who trusts Jesus.

Here's the promise—notice how many times God says,
"I will":

"They will be my people, and *I will* be their God. *I will*
give them singleness of heart and action, so that they
will always fear me and that all will then go well for

them and for their children after them. *I will* make an
everlasting covenant with them: *I will* never stop doing
good to them, and *I will* inspire them to fear me, so
that they will never turn away from me. *I will* rejoice in
doing them good and *will* assuredly plant them in this
land with all my heart and soul."

(Jeremiah 32 v 38-41, italics mine)

Let's enjoy the "I wills".

"I will give them singleness of heart." God promises to give
his people an unbroken, undivided heart: a heart that trusts
and loves and fears God alone. In place of our many hearts
with many loves, God will give us (literally) "one heart", with
one love. Instead of each room in our heart hosting a different
squatter, now the whole house will be devoted to one resident
owner: Jesus. God has promised to give you and me integrity
and literal wholeheartedness.

"They will always fear me." Our new, undivided hearts will
have one desire in life—to always fear God. God's liberation
strategy for a heart that is torn by many fears is to unite that
heart with one fear—fear of him. While my other fears enslave
me in selfishness, fearing God alone liberates me to do what
is right, because the God who rules the universe will never
stop doing good to me. And while my other fears cause my
heart to disintegrate, fearing God alone mends me because
God can deal with every situation, so my whole heart can
stand in awe of him, bringing integrity to my life.

"I will inspire them to fear me." What will produce this
liberating awe of God in our hearts? On either side of God's
promise to inspire us to fear him, he makes an identical
promise: "I will never stop doing good to them ... I will rejoice
in doing them good." God's goodness to us is what inspires us
to stand in awe of him. How is God doing good to us? Here are

some ways, all taken from Romans 8. Take a moment to slowly read and pray through them. Reflect on God's promises, and let his goodness inspire your heart to be awed by him:

- God will never condemn you, because he condemned your sin in his Son, Jesus, instead (v 1-4).
- God gives you his Spirit to live in you and to give you life and peace and righteousness (v 5-10).
- God will raise you from the dead to live with him for ever, just as he has already raised Christ (v 11-13).
- God has adopted you—you share the same Father, same Spirit and same inheritance as Jesus (v 14-17).
- God has given you the certain hope of sharing in Jesus' freedom and glory in the new creation (v 18-25).
- God's Spirit helps you to pray in your struggles, when you're groaning and don't know what to say (v 26-27).
- God uses all things—even hard and painful things— for your ultimate good (v 28).
- Before time began, God loved you and chose you to be a member of his family, and now is working to change you to be more and more like your big brother, Jesus (v 29-30).
- God has declared you innocent and beautiful in his sight and he will never stop loving you (v 31-34).
- Nothing you do, and nothing done to you, will ever separate you from God's infinite and eternal love for you (v 35-39).

Awesome! And that's just one chapter from a whole Bible of God's goodness... what a God!

"I will rejoice in doing them good." God radiates so brightly with kindness and undeserved grace that he enjoys doing good to weak, flawed, failing sinners like you and me. He saves us "with all [his] heart and soul".

You will love God with an undivided heart when you see that he loves you with an undivided heart. He doesn't love you reluctantly or half-heartedly. He doesn't love you because he has to. He certainly doesn't love you because you've done anything to deserve it. He loves loving you. He gets a kick out of it. Nothing thrills God more than doing good to people who have been doing evil. Doesn't that in itself inspire you to fear and love him?

A prayer of broken hearts

Psalm 86 shows us more of how our broken hearts can be mended:

"Among the gods there is none like you, Lord;
   no deeds can compare with yours.
All the nations you have made
   will come and worship before you, Lord;
   they will bring glory to your name.
For you are great and do marvellous deeds;
   you alone are God.
Teach me your way, LORD,
   that I may rely on your faithfulness;
give me an undivided heart,
   that I may fear your name.
I will praise you, Lord my God, with all my heart;
   I will glorify your name for ever.
For great is your love towards me;
   you have delivered me from the depths,
   from the realm of the dead." (Psalm 86 v 8-13)

These verses show the same logic that we saw in the greatest commandment. There is only one God. No other gods compare to him; because he alone made all the nations, he alone deserves all honour and glory. So David prays for a heart that reflects this reality: an "undivided heart" that fears and worships God alone. He takes the Hebrew number "one" and turns it into a verb: *One-ify my heart, so that I may fear your name.*

We need to remember that this psalm is not an essay in a theology exam. The rest of the psalm shows how desperate David's situation is. His life is in danger (v 2); he's crying out to God in distress (v 7); ruthless enemies are trying to kill him (v 14). He's in exactly the sort of situation where we naturally get afraid and look for an escape. The only other way is to live out of an "undivided heart" that fears God's name (v 11). And by the very next verse God is answering his prayer: "I will praise you, Lord my God, with all my heart" (v 12).

We fight fear with fear. We combat the fears that enslave us with the fear of God that liberates us. Only God can inspire this kind of awe of himself in us. Only God can cause us to escape our escapism. If you think that the words of this book will change you automatically, or if you mistake this for a self-help book that's encouraging you to improve yourself, then any change will be shallow and short-lived. Reading this book won't help you at all unless you are praying Psalm 86 v 11 for yourself. So add it to your prayer diary, stick it on your fridge, print it on a T-shirt, get it inked into your arm—whatever you need to do to prompt yourself to pray like David:

"Teach me your way, LORD,
    that I may rely on your faithfulness;
give me an undivided heart,
    that I may fear your name."

Pictures of God

Psalm 86 tells us to pray. It also tells us to picture. David reminds himself that the incomparable God is "my God" (v 2, 12). He knows that the God of the universe is personally committed to him, and David is personally committed to the God of the universe. To use the biblical language, he is in a "covenant" with God.

When someone describes a person they love, they often use a picture to sum up what that person means to them:

"You are my sunshine."

"She is my anchor."

"He is my world."

Throughout his psalms, David does the same with God. Who is God to you, David?

"He is my refuge."

"He is my rock."

"He is my shepherd."

And many more.

By using all of these different pictures to describe his relationship with God, David is remembering that his God is God in and over all of life. Whatever the problem, God is his solution. Whatever the question, God is his answer. Whatever the danger, God is his first resort. David doesn't just trust his Lord for forgiveness and eternal life; he trusts the Lord for everything in this life. These pictures sum up that trust and help him to live out that trust.

These pictures can be God's tools in restoring our hearts too. They stimulate our imagination. They stir our hearts. They stick in our memories. They show us Jesus from new angles, so we can see how all-sufficient he is. They help us to be more in awe of him, and less in awe of anything else. Gazing on these pictures in our minds and hearts helps us to live them out in real life. As we'll see, none of them are totally separate to the others, and for any one area in which you excel at escaping, there'll probably be three or four of the pictures that you could use to combat your escapism. But applying these pictures of Jesus to your heart is the key to your heart being united, and to your escapist days being through:

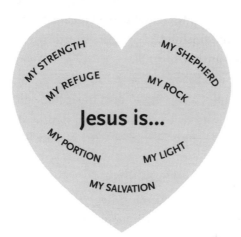

MY STRENGTH
MY SHEPHERD
MY REFUGE
MY ROCK
Jesus is...
MY PORTION
MY LIGHT
MY SALVATION

It may seem odd to go to some Iron Age poetry in the Old Testament to help us to live as New Testament Christians. But these psalms are for us, because they are the prayers of Christ. They are prayers of faith in Christ, because the Lord whom the psalm-writers were fearing, loving and praising around 3,000 years ago is the Lord who walked this earth 2,000 years ago. They are also prayers of the faith of Christ: Jesus prayed these psalms, because he was a man supremely and perfectly committed to fearing, loving and praising his Father with all his heart. These pictures show us Jesus. And they help us to pray like, love like, and live like Jesus.

All you need to move forward

So every chapter in the rest of this book will focus on one of these pictures, as we ask God to begin restoring and uniting our rundown, divided hearts. We'll look at what it means to see Jesus in the centre of each of these pictures—as all we need to move forwards and move upwards in life, even when the path is hard.

In using these pictures of who Jesus is for you, you're not trying to do anything new. You already know how to make something your refuge or your light—you do it every time you put off a job on your to-do list or worry about what someone will think of a decision you've got to make. Every escapist is already an expert at having a rock, a portion, and so on. All you need to do is switch from making false gods into your light and your strength to having Jesus as your light and your strength instead. Yes, you'll need the power of God's Spirit to do that. But no, it's not complicated.

All you'll be doing is repenting. Repentance is good news, not the downside of the Christian life (which is how we often see it). Our old refuges and rocks lead us to avoid difficult people, put off difficult challenges and give up in difficult times. They enslave us and cause our hearts to divide. But Jesus is a better refuge, a better rock. With him we can love difficult people, tackle difficult challenges and persevere in difficult times. He makes us strong and courageous. He liberates us and mends our hearts. Repentance is switching from fearing gods who can't help and don't deliver to living in joyful awe of the God to whom we owe everything and for whom we were made. Repentance is trading a compromised life that doesn't work for a committed, courageous life that does.

So let's get on to looking at these pictures, and see how much better Jesus is.

4. Refuge

"The LORD is my refuge."
Psalm 91 v 9

Harlech Castle in Wales holds an impressive record. Between 1461 and 1468 it endured the longest siege in British history, holding out against an army of 9,000 men. By the end, it was the only place in the whole of England or Wales that the House of York, one of the families vying for control of the throne, did not control.

Even today, Harlech is an awe-inspiring fortress. It perches on a rock nearly 200 feet high. The concentric walls are 40 feet tall and over 10 feet thick. Back in the fifteenth century, it could only be entered across a narrow stone bridge and through a gatehouse with three portcullises. Arrow slits, battlements and murder holes also helped to keep the home insurance premiums down.

The castle was built by the English when they invaded Wales. Subduing the Welsh was a dangerous task. But when the locals were restless, the English soldiers could take refuge in their castle rather than escaping back to England. They could complete the difficult mission they had been given.

When we're tempted to escape, we need a refuge like that castle. We need somewhere that will enable us to keep doing the difficult things we're meant to do.

Psalm 11 tells us where our castle is located:

"In the LORD I take refuge.
   How then can you say to me:
   'Flee like a bird to your mountain?'" (Psalm 11 v 1)

As he wrote these words, David was under attack, outnumbered and in danger. But with the Lord as his refuge, he didn't need to escape. And with the Lord as your refuge, you won't need to either.

How to choose your refuge

In 1000 BC, when David was composing his psalms, they didn't have castles. But they did have Iron Age hill forts. When an army invaded, instead of running away, everyone would run to the fortress and take refuge there. Then they could stay where they were until the threat had passed. There was no need to escape as refugees to another land.

What makes a good fortress? First, it needs to be strong. It must defend you from whatever and whoever is threatening you. The hill it stands on must be steep; the walls must be thick and high; the gate must be heavily defended. It must be secure.

Second, it needs to be loving—that is, loyal. It must be on your side. It must be committed to welcoming you. A secure fortress is no help if the gates are shut when you arrive. If the garrison hold a grudge against you, or look out for themselves before others, or are prone to switching their allegiance, you can't depend on it as your stronghold.

If you don't have a strong, loving refuge, then you get

caught in open ground. In David's day, that might mean facing soldiers with swords and chariots. In your day, it will be your fears. And when your life is full of fear and empty of refuge, your only options are the three instinctive human reactions to fear: fight, flight or freeze.

To fight means rolling up your sleeves, gritting your teeth and trying your hardest to confront your problems yourself. You won't manage to keep that up for long when a fearsome army comes to besiege you; and lashing out often hurts those closest to you. Sooner rather than later, and leaving a likely trail of destruction, you're left with only options two or three.

You might choose flight—running away, and leaving the hard things you ought to do undone. You put off difficult tasks, avoid difficult people and give up in difficult times. The battle is lost before it has even begun.

Or you may just freeze. This is when panic sets in and you feel paralysed. It's doing nothing and hoping the problem goes away. You don't win any battles with this tactic either. Wishful thinking never defeated any problem.

If, on the other hand, you find a refuge that is strong and loving, then it's a different story. You confront a challenge from behind a moat, a strong wall and towering battlements. If your strong refuge is for you, it doesn't matter who is against you. There is no need to escape, and no reason to panic. You can stick around and keep struggling on, and on, and on, for even longer than the seven years the men of Harlech managed.

That's the difference a refuge makes.

Christ is your refuge

The only refuge that is strong enough and loving enough is Christ. This is how David responded in Psalm 59 when he was surrounded by enemies:

"But I will sing of your strength,
   in the morning I will sing of your love;
for you are my fortress,
   my refuge in times of trouble.
You are my strength, I sing praise to you;
   you, God, are my fortress,
   my God on whom I can rely." (Psalm 59 v 16-17)

Even under threat, David sang! He sang because God was his fortress, his refuge, his castle. He sang of God's strength, because his castle was strong enough to repel any attack. He sang of God's love, because God would never be disloyal to him. Like a soldier taunting a besieging army from the top of an impregnable castle wall, David could joyfully sing when we would probably just get stressed.

Psalm 62 underlines the point:

"Trust in him at all times, you people;
   pour out your hearts to him,
   for God is our refuge." (Psalm 62 v 8)

And what makes God such a wonderful refuge?

"One thing God has spoken,
   two things I have heard:
'Power belongs to you, God,
   and with you, Lord, is unfailing love.'"

                                    (Psalm 62 v 11-12)

No power is like God's power—his "incomparably great power" which is always available "for us who believe" (Ephesians 1 v 19). It raised Christ from the dead—it can take you through life (Ephesians 1 v 20-21). God's strength is stronger than any enemy you face, even death. He is a strong refuge.

No love is like God's love. He has demonstrated his love

to us once and for all by sending Christ to die for us while we were still guilty sinners (Romans 5 v 8). Because of his great love for us, he has made us alive with Christ and has saved us by his lavish grace (Ephesians 2 v 4-5). God's love is unfailing—he will never leave us in the lurch, and he will never hold our sins against us. The door is never closed against us. He is a welcoming refuge.

Christ is the ultimate source of homeland security. With him as our castle, we never need to escape. Which is all well and good, but... Christ is not actually a castle. So what does it look like to "take refuge in him"—and what are we taking refuge from?

In him, from him

The first reference in the psalms to God's Son, the Christ, being our refuge is a surprise. We don't only take refuge in Christ; we also take refuge in Christ from Christ. The biggest threat to us isn't the problems we face or the people we fear; it's Christ himself.

In Psalm 2, the kings of the earth are revolting—against God. They think life under God's rule is a matter of "chains" and "shackles", and they want to choose their own purpose in life, live by their own values and follow their own dreams (v 1-3).

In one sense, God doesn't take this rebellion seriously: he "laughs" at the idea that they could overthrow him (v 4). But in another sense, he does take it very seriously: he "rebukes them in his anger", because they are mounting a coup against his Son, Jesus, who he has "installed [as] king" even over "the ends of the earth" (v 5-6, 8).

And so the psalm ends with some words of warning and advice for these kings. They need to find a refuge from the wrath of God's anointed King, Jesus:

"Therefore, you kings, be wise;
　be warned, you rulers of the earth.
Serve the LORD with fear
　and celebrate his rule with trembling.
Kiss his son, or he will be angry
　and your way will lead to your destruction,
for his wrath can flare up in a moment.
　Blessed are all who take refuge in him." (v 10-12)

We need to hear these words of warning too. We may not be recognised as kings and queens by anyone else, but we all try to be kings and queens of our own lives. We often feel it would deprive us of our freedom and rights and happiness to live the way Jesus tells us. We've all mounted a coup in our hearts against God. So the wrath of God that threatened those kings threatens us too. The anger of God's Son, Jesus, is the biggest danger any of us will ever face. The main peril we need to take refuge from is Christ himself.

But wonderfully, this same psalm tells us to take refuge from Christ by taking refuge in Christ. We're saved from his wrath not by running away from him (which is impossible—it's hard to outrun the omnipresent God), but by running to him: "Blessed are all who take refuge in him" (v 12). Christ became our refuge on the cross. When the Son of God died, the wrath of God "flare[d] up" and consumed him, so that it need not consume us.

I once ran an event at church for dads and their kids where we invited the local fire brigade along. They brought one of their engines, which caused great excitement (mainly among the dads). One guy asked if they had ever lost a fire engine. A fireman told us about the time a crew had gone to put out a fire in a field. They had parked the engine and unrolled the hoses, and then the wind changed direction and the fire consumed the engine before they had time to drive out of the way.

"Stupid idiots," said the fireman. "They should have parked on the patch that was already burned."

Fire can't burn the same patch of ground twice. Firemen know that. It's the same with God's wrath—he'll only punish each act of rebellion once. When Jesus died on the cross and God's wrath fell on him, he created a patch of ground where God's wrath has already burned. So the only safe place to take refuge is there—in him, at his cross. "Take refuge in him" (v 12).

If you haven't heard this before, or haven't believed it before, you must start here. If you haven't grasped that Christ died to be your refuge from Christ, then the rest of this book will never come alive for you. Your attempts to be strong and courageous will be flawed from the start. You might do it to prove yourself to God in a proud but desperate bid to persuade him to accept you. Or you will do it to prove yourself to the people around you so that they respect and admire you. Or you'll be doing it to prove yourself to yourself, using Christ to feel better about yourself and to make your life more manageable and successful.

These motives are all weak and self-centred. Before you can experience true freedom, you need to be both cast down and lifted up by the conviction that Christ is your refuge from Christ. You must start here.

But if you have heard this before (many times, perhaps), and have believed it before, you must not stop here. Christ is our refuge from Christ, but he's also our refuge from everything else that threatens us too.

There have been times in my life when I've trusted Jesus to save me from his wrath when I die, but day by day I've lived as if it's down to me to deal with the rest of my problems by myself. I've felt that Christ will protect me one day, but not this day. That's when I've given in to fear and looked for an escape.

But marvellously, Christ is more than just a refuge from Christ; he's a refuge for us in all our problems and struggles. I'm not saying this to add to the gospel; I'm saying it because the gospel is bigger than we've imagined, and Christ is better than we've ever dreamed.

Christ is your refuge... when you're attacked

When you take on a new role at work and you're criticised by a jealous colleague... or when you take a stand against the way a group gossips and snipes, and you become the target of the gossiping and sniping... or when your church works for justice in your community and you get threatened by local vested interests... you feel vulnerable. You want to run away and hide.

The prophet Jeremiah knew that feeling. He had a ridiculously hard job—telling God's people that God was going to judge them. For his troubles he was mocked and criticised, threatened and bullied, imprisoned and beaten up. His life was full of despair and disaster. But he kept going— because God was his refuge:

> "I have not run away from being your shepherd;
>   you know I have not desired the day of despair.
>   What passes my lips is open before you.
> Do not be a terror to me;
>   you are my refuge in the day of disaster."

(Jeremiah 17 v 16-17)

The reason that Jeremiah didn't run away was that he had a refuge. He knew that the Lord was his strong and loyal castle. Behind the ramparts and the battlements he could endure the siege. Behind those walls, you too can keep living with courage when people are opposing you.

Christ is your refuge... when you're afraid

If we have a refuge, then fight, flight or freeze aren't the only options when we're afraid. The psalms give us a fourth option: faith.

"When I am afraid, I put my trust in you.
In God, whose word I praise—
in God I trust and am not afraid.
What can mere mortals do to me?" (Psalm 56 v 3-4)

Nehemiah is a great example of this. A member of God's people in exile, he was cupbearer to the all-powerful Persian King Artaxerxes, and wanted his permission to help his own people rebuild Jerusalem. But to approach the king was a risk—the king could refuse, or possibly even take this as an insult and have him put to death. The king spotted Nehemiah's sadness, and wanted to know the cause. And with great bravery (and urgent prayer) Nehemiah told him. Nehemiah puts it this way:

"I was very much afraid, but I said to the king, 'May the king live for ever! Why should my face not look sad when the city where my ancestors are buried lies in ruins, and its gates have been destroyed by fire?'"

(Nehemiah 2 v 2-3)

"I was very much afraid, but..." It's possible to feel fear and yet neither freeze nor fight nor flee. Nehemiah overcame his fear because he'd spent the last four months praying and fasting and making God his refuge. So here's the wonderful truth: you can feel afraid, but it doesn't have to dominate and direct you, to paralyse you or hold you back. With faith in God as

your refuge, you can feel afraid and still do bold and risky things for God and his people.

Christ is your refuge… when you're alone

We all know how hard it is to be brave and to do the right thing when we feel unsupported and isolated. When you're the only Christian at a party… when you're the only carer for an elderly parent… when you're booking a table for one… when everyone else has gone to bed and the web is your oyster… that's when it is often hardest to do what is best rather than what is easy.

Or to put it as David did:

"Look and see, there is no one at my right hand;
  no one is concerned for me.
I have no refuge;
  no one cares for my life.
I cry to you, LORD;
  I say, 'You are my refuge,
  my portion in the land of the living.'" (Psalm 142 v 4-5)

When we have no other refuge, the Lord is our refuge. He is concerned for us, and stays at our right hand. Instead of running away from our responsibilities, we can run to Jesus who gives us strength and courage when we're alone.

That's what the widow and refugee Ruth discovered. She took brave decisions because of her faith in God: she trusted God to provide when her husband died; she left her homeland and her family's religion to follow her mother-in-law, Naomi, to the famine-struck land of Canaan; she stuck by her when Naomi lashed out in bitterness and despair; she went gleaning in the fields alone when she knew that an immigrant woman like her could be assaulted. The book of Ruth is about a woman refusing to be driven by fear.

Where did this bravery come from? From her faith that the God of Israel was her refuge. As her future husband, Boaz, put it:

> "May you be richly rewarded by the LORD, the God of Israel, under whose wings you have come to take refuge." (Ruth 2 v 12)

Taking refuge in Christ

If you have a strong and loving refuge, then there is no need to escape or to lash out when you are attacked, afraid or alone. Walk by faith in the Lord as your refuge, and you won't get caught in open ground.

To see what this will look like for you, try answering these questions and praying about your answers.

1. *When are you tempted to escape?* When do you fear that you will be attacked if you stand up for what is right and just? Maybe you fear an overbearing parent, or a critical boss, or a blame culture at work. Perhaps there are situations where it is easier to remain silent, or not try anything new, because you'd become a target for people's verbal arrows.

When are you afraid, and likely to fight, flee or freeze? For a student, it might be when a difficult essay needs writing; for a parent, it might be when a difficult child is playing up; for a pastor, it might be when a difficult church member needs confronting; for a manager, it might be when a difficult decision needs making. Perhaps it's when you have to try something new, or when you know there's a risk of failure.

When do you feel alone and unsupported? Maybe there's a role that you're tired of doing on your own, or a time in the day when no one is watching, or a situation where you are the only person around who loves Jesus.

Try to identify and write down particular places, or times in the week, when you need Jesus to be your refuge.

2. What escape do you turn to? Think about where you run to when you're caught in open ground. An employee putting off work might turn to her Twitter feed or an internet survey telling her what Star Wars character she is. Her boss might simultaneously be taking refuge in work, staying late to avoid problems at home. A parent avoiding engaging with their children might flick through Facebook on their phone, hide in the shed, or slump the kids in front of a screen for hours on end. A husband struggling with a depressed wife might escape to porn sites, betting shops or a hotel where he's away from the stresses and responsibilities.

None of these may be you—but you will have your own favoured escape routes. What are they? What do you do instead of loving those difficult people, tacking those difficult challenges and persevering through those difficult times?

3. What will it mean to make Jesus your refuge at those times? What Bible verses that describe how strong and loving Jesus is could you write out and stick up in helpful places, or memorise for when you need them? When do you need to run to Jesus in prayer and rely on him? What would you think, say and do differently if you lived by faith when you feel afraid?

Christ is not just your refuge

Every time I take to the hills, I have my bivvy bag with me. It's an orange plastic sleeping bag that will keep me warm and dry if I get injured or caught overnight. It's my portable refuge. But I've never used it. It just stays folded up in the bottom of my bag.

There is a danger in thinking of Jesus as our refuge. We can treat him like I treat my bivvy bag—handy in a crisis, but irrelevant the rest of the time. He becomes our comfort blanket. We assume that he will be there for us, and we forget that we are here for him. We use him, but we don't stand in awe of him.

I hope you've found it good to realise that the Lord Jesus is your refuge. But you must also appreciate that he isn't just your refuge. That's why we need to remember we take refuge from Christ as well as in Christ. And that's why we need the other pictures that God gives us to unite our hearts in awed fear of him alone.

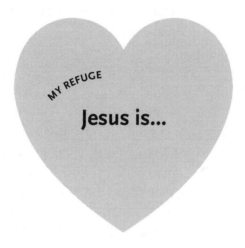

5. Shepherd

"The LORD is my shepherd."
Psalm 23 v 1

If escapism were a sport at the Olympics, John Darwin would win gold.

When Darwin ran up large debts buying and renting houses, he concluded the best way out was to fake his own death so that his wife Anne could claim on his life insurance. On 21st March 2002, he paddled his canoe into the North Sea and disappeared. He spent the next few years hiding in a secret apartment accessed through the false back of a wardrobe before trying to start a new life in Panama. It was five years before the scam was discovered. John and Anne's deceit was splashed across the front pages, and both of them were convicted of fraud and sent to prison.

John Darwin is an extreme example. But it shows that although escapism promises us a way out of our problems, it only makes those problems worse. So hiding away at home and not answering the phone when we've fallen out with someone makes it even harder to patch up the relationship. Telling a lie to escape the blame for a mistake tends to cause deeper trouble later on. Being defensive and avoiding talking about our struggles makes it even harder to cope with them. Playing games online or on the Xbox, because that world seems easier than facing the real one, just stops us getting to grips with life, and does nothing to erase the nagging sense that we're just treading water.

One of the Bible's descriptions for people like us is that we're "sheep without a shepherd" (Numbers 27 v 17). It's not meant to be a compliment. Left to ourselves we make stupid, short-term decisions that make things easier now and worse tomorrow. We take easy paths that lead to bad places, instead of following difficult paths that lead to good places.

Sheep need a shepherd. And so do we. We need someone to tell us which path leads to true freedom and contentment; and we need someone to lead us to that place through whatever difficulties lie in the way.

So when the Lord Jesus proclaims, "I am the good shepherd" (John 10 v 11, 14), it's great news for escapists. Here is a shepherd who promises us security and protection if we listen to his voice and follow him.

To see what makes Jesus such a good shepherd, we need look at Psalm 23. It's another of King David's greatest hits. David had been a shepherd himself, so he knows what he's talking about. It's a justly famous psalm that will probably be read at your funeral, but you need its message for life now. Bang in the centre of the poem is a phrase escapists long to say:

"Even though I walk
through the darkest valley,
I will fear no evil." (Psalm 23 v 4)

You can be fearless too, if you follow Jesus as your shepherd. Psalm 23 shows us four reasons why.

1. Green pastures

England is renowned as a green and pleasant land, because it has plenty of hills with plenty of rain producing plenty of lush green grass. This makes life easy for sheep, but difficult for English people like me to hear the wonder in David's voice as he sings:

> "The LORD is my shepherd, I lack nothing.
>   He makes me lie down in green pastures,
> he leads me beside quiet waters." (v 1-2)

Green pastures may be nothing special in England, but in the Middle East, where David lived, they are gold dust. The grass is only green for three months each year. Each day a flock needs their shepherd to lead them to somewhere where they can graze. Sheep only settle down to rest when they have a full stomach.

Fresh drinking water is also easier to find in England than in the Middle East. There, sheep need their shepherd to find a reliable source of water in the middle of the day. And that water must be still, because sheep will not drink from running water.

Green pastures, still water... what meticulous care David's shepherd lavishes on him! Only with a kind and skilful shepherd will a sheep in Israel "lack nothing" (v 1). But that's the kind of shepherd David has. And the Lord goes even further in his tenderness:

> "He tends his flock like a shepherd:
>   he gathers the lambs in his arms
> and carries them close to his heart;
>   he gently leads those that have young." (Isaiah 40 v 11)

Each lambing season, my dad used to head up to Scotland to help some friends of ours who were sheep farmers. He would do night shifts in the lambing shed, helping ewes to give birth and bond with their lambs. In school holidays I would stay on the farm too. One time Alistair, the farmer, brought in a tiny newborn lamb that was struggling. He let me help him cuddle it, warm it up by the radiator and feed it with a bottle until it was well enough to be returned to its mother. That, says Isaiah, is the gentleness that the Lord has for each one of us.

It's why the Lord came to earth—to be our shepherd. As Jesus looked on the large crowds that had followed him into the wilderness, he had "compassion on them, because they were like sheep without a shepherd" (Mark 6 v 34). So he became their shepherd: he taught them, feeding them with his word; then he settled them down "on the green grass" (Mark 6 v 39) and fed all 5000 of them with bread and fish.

It's crucial to know what a shepherd is, and who our shepherd is, because our shepherd often tells us to do things that are far more difficult than not doing them. Sometimes he prompts us to do things that we think will mess up our lives. In his word, he calls us to work diligently (e.g. 2 Thessalonians 3 v 7-13), but we will often feel that holding down a job, or going the extra mile for a colleague, or signing up for a ministry at church will take away our rest. He calls us to bear one another's burdens (Galatians 6 v 2), but of course getting alongside a difficult or hurting person in order to support and love them will rob us of our time, our energy, and quite possibly our peace. He calls us to only marry someone who is a fellow believer and who will support us as we seek to follow him (1 Corinthians 7 v 39), but turning down or ending a relationship that is dragging us away from Christ makes us worry we will end up lonely and childless. He calls us to stand up for the abused and stand against injustice—but doing that in our workplace or in our community looks like the path to unpopularity and poverty.

Jesus calls us to a life that is much more difficult than a life without him. But Jesus is a good shepherd, and the grass is greener on his side. A sheep that ignores its shepherd's call and stays in its pen will never enjoy the lush pastures and still waters. Only by listening to our shepherd's voice and following him out of our comfort zone will we find true rest and peace.

2. Search and rescue

How else does having Jesus as our shepherd help us to be fearless?

"He refreshes my soul.
He guides me along the right paths
    for his name's sake." (Psalm 23 v 3)

In this translation, we might read the first phrase as a promise of a relaxing break at a spa hotel. But it's written as the counterpoint to the second half of the verse. Kenneth Bailey, a biblical scholar who has spent years in the Middle East, translates it more literally and helpfully as, "He brings me back" or even, "He causes me to repent".

Sheep have a tendency to wander into the wrong paths. So do we—we stray from our shepherd and get ourselves stuck. When this happens, like sheep, we are hopeless at rescuing ourselves. We need our shepherd to find us and to bring us back. We're responsible for getting ourselves lost; the shepherd is responsible for finding us.

It turns out that "Little Bo Peep" was not written by a shepherd. Leave us alone, and we won't come home. Sheep don't save themselves. They need a search-and-rescue mission:

> "I myself will tend my sheep and make them lie down,
> declares the Sovereign LORD. I will search for the lost
> and bring back the strays." (Ezekiel 34 v 15-16)

We hear more of this rescue operation in the parable Jesus told to people who criticised his choice of companions.

> "Suppose one of you has a hundred sheep and loses
> one of them. Doesn't he leave the ninety-nine in the
> open country and go after the lost sheep until he
> finds it? And when he finds it, he joyfully puts it on his
> shoulders and goes home. Then he calls his friends and
> neighbours together and says, 'Rejoice with me; I have
> found my lost sheep.' I tell you that in the same way
> there will be more rejoicing in heaven over one sinner
> who repents than over ninety-nine righteous people
> who do not need to repent." (Luke 15 v 4-7)

Jesus our shepherd spares no effort to bring back his sheep and care for us. He left his throne in heaven, became a human being, endured rejection and ridicule, suffered and died, for what? To find his lost sheep. Jesus our shepherd cares for each individual in his flock. Each and every sinner matters. Even if you had been the only sinner in the whole world, Jesus would still have come and died, just for you!

There is no shortage of advice when you're in trouble. Whether it is well-meaning friends, agony aunts, self-help books, life coaches or YouTube videos, there are plenty of applicants for the role of your shepherd. But only one shepherd died for you. Only one shepherd can be trusted, time and time again, to bring you back and cause you to repent so that you can walk along the right paths. Those paths may look steep and rocky to you, but Jesus is a reliable guide.

3. Rod and staff

As well as being a danger to themselves, sheep also face dangers from other creatures. Since they have no claws or teeth or tusks to protect themselves, what can they do when they are threatened?

"Even though I walk
  through the darkest valley,
I will fear no evil,
  for you are with me;
your rod and your staff,
  they comfort me.
You prepare a table before me
  in the presence of my enemies.
You anoint my head with oil;
  my cup overflows." (Psalm 23 v 4-5)

Is there a place you are scared to go to? David speaks of walking "through the darkest valley". Are there people you are nervous to be around? David sits "in the presence of [his] enemies". Yet even here, David can be fearless—and so can you, because Jesus your shepherd is with you, and he is holding his rod and his staff.

The "rod" was a shepherd's weapon for defending the sheep. It was a club, a bit like a mace, often with shards of iron embedded in the end. When a wolf or lion or bear or thief attacked, the shepherd's rod was what he used to defend his sheep.

Defending your sheep is still a core part of shepherding today. James Rebanks is a shepherd in the Lake District who writes books and tweets (@herdyshepherd1) about his way of life. This is what he writes about other people's dogs:

> "Keep your dog away from other people's sheep and it is none of our business. Let it loose, so it begins to chase them or worse, and you have put your dog in the path of a bullet. Shepherds have always had a legal right to protect their flocks. Faced with a rogue dog, we have a right, and a kind of duty, to shoot it."
>
> (*A Shepherd's Life*, pages 124-125)

A good shepherd carries the weapons to protect his sheep from anything that might hurt them. Jesus has a rod—he protects you with the same sense of duty and determination.

The "staff" was a lighter, longer stick, like a modern-day shepherd's crook. It was used for guiding sheep, keeping them on the path, and lifting them over obstacles. This is how the shepherd guided his sheep through the dangerous places he took them to in order to lead them safely to pasture.

We might wish that Jesus would never lead us through dark valleys or feed us in dangerous company. But that's where Psalm 23 says he will lead us. Jesus won't take you round your troubles; he'll take you through them. Only by guiding you through those dark places can he teach you to rely on him completely. Only as you look back at the path that he led you on through the dark do you learn that you can follow him with complete trust and total joy, even when the path meanders and night falls. You might want to use Jesus to change your difficult circumstances, but Jesus wants to use your difficult circumstances to change you. And he'll walk with you every step of the way.

So think of that place where you are scared to go—your "valley of the shadow of death", as the older translations of Psalm 23 put it. Maybe there's an "alley of the shadow of death" in your area. Perhaps it's your workplace or somewhere with bad memories. Remember that when you go there, Jesus your shepherd is with you. Picture his rod and his staff. Even in that place, there is no need for your life to be directed or dominated by fear.

Or think of those people who make you nervous—the gang of youths, the threatening neighbour, the bullying colleague, the overbearing relative. When you meet them, be assured that Jesus your shepherd is with you. Look at his rod and his staff. Don't let the fear take over. Let your awe-filled faith in the shepherd be bigger than your fear of the valley.

There will be days—and maybe today is one of them—when you need to remember that Jesus says this about himself, and about you:

> "I am the good shepherd. The good shepherd lays down his life for the sheep. The hired hand is not the shepherd and does not own the sheep. So when he sees the wolf coming, he abandons the sheep and runs away. Then the wolf attacks the flock and scatters it. The man runs away because he is a hired hand and cares nothing for the sheep. I am the good shepherd." (John 10 v 11-14)

Of all the enemies we face, none are scarier than Satan. Of all the dark places where we might go, none are more terrifying than death. Yet Jesus has laid down his life to protect us from both of these wolves. His death in our place has removed the sting of death for us. On the cross he defeated Satan and stripped him of his weapons by taking away our sin and our guilt. We are eternally secure and protected. Nothing in the future can terrify Jesus' sheep:

> "My sheep listen to my voice; I know them, and they follow me. I give them eternal life, and they shall never perish; no one will snatch them out of my hand. My Father, who has given them to me, is greater than all;

no one can snatch them out of my Father's hand. I and
the Father are one." (John 10 v 27-30)

4. Chase scene

Every time you leave your house, you are being followed.
Wherever you run, you will be chased. Wherever you hide, you
will be found. This pursuit is relentless, and will never end.

That might sound disturbing, but look who is doing the
following:

"Surely your goodness and love will follow me
   all the days of my life,
and I will dwell in the house of the LORD
   for ever." (Psalm 23 v 6)

David knows that he enjoys eternal security—he will dwell
in God's house for ever. But he also knows he enjoys present
security each day in this life—every day, his Lord's goodness
and love are following him wherever he goes. Here are two of
the Bible's favourite words to describe God: "goodness" refers to
God's unalloyed moral and relational beauty; "love" denotes the
loyalty, faithfulness and undeserved kindness God consistently
shows towards his people. That's who is following you.

In fact, it's even stronger than that. Literally, David says
that God's goodness and love will "pursue" him—it's actually
the same Hebrew word that was used of Pharaoh chasing
the Israelites as they escaped from Egypt in Exodus 14. God's
goodness and love act like two sheepdogs running after us to
keep us safe.

This is a wonderful truth. The Bible often talks about the
Christian life as one of following Jesus; but this psalm tells
us that it is just as much about Jesus following us. You might
have heard people saying that faith is about our pursuit of

God; really, it is about God's pursuit of us. Wherever you go, whatever you do, however you feel and whatever scrapes you get yourself into, if the Lord is your shepherd, then his goodness and love will be on your tail every step of the way.

Again, this gives steel to our faith when Jesus leads us outside of our comfort zone. If he calls you to go to another country as a missionary, or to remain single for the gospel, or to join a church plant, or to set up a Christian Union at your school, or to speak up for Jesus at work, then he also promises that his goodness and love will pursue you as you do it. He calls you to do hard things, but he never fails to equip you or be with you in those hard things. Whatever difficult and dangerous-looking journey Jesus leads you on, his grace will be with you every step of the way. And what more could you want or need or ask for?

Listening to Jesus' voice

In the Middle East, shepherds often bring their flocks together at night for protection. When they go their separate ways, each shepherd has a special call or a tune on their flute. Every sheep knows its shepherd's voice, and will follow him out to the pastures.

Jesus says that being his sheep is a matter of listening to his voice and following him:

> "[The shepherd] calls his own sheep by name and leads
> them out. When he has brought out all his own, he
> goes on ahead of them, and his sheep follow him
> because they know his voice." (John 10 v 3-4)

We hear Jesus' voice every time we open our Bible or hear a faithful sermon. Through his word, Jesus leads us and calls us to follow him; and through his Spirit he prompts us to follow in specific situations. And following him in obedience will normally be tougher than not following him. That is when we need to remember from Psalm 23 that Jesus' guidance is much better than ours or anyone else's.

- When you've fallen out with someone, Jesus calls you to make the first move to mend the relationship, whoever's fault it was (see Matthew 5 v 23-24 when it's your fault, and 18 v 15 when it's theirs!). When you want to take the easy way out by avoiding the other person, or pretending that nothing has happened while seething underneath, you need to remember that you'll only enjoy the green pastures of a clean conscience and deep relationships if you listen to what Jesus says. Obeying him is harder, but it's better.
- When you make a mistake or break a promise, Jesus guides you by calling you to repentance. If you choose to save face by covering it up or making excuses, you'll miss out on his search-and-rescue mission. Owning up will take courage, but only by following Jesus will you walk unburdened, in the paths of integrity and truth. Obeying him is harder, but it's better.
- When you're walking through a dark valley, struggling with difficulties like debt or despair or depression, Jesus promises to walk with you. He'll carry you when he has to. Often his presence and help come through his people. Opening up to a trusted Christian friend about your struggles might feel as if it is making you more vulnerable, but it is actually often Jesus' way of protecting you. Obeying him is harder, but it's better.
- When you're anxious about the way the Spirit seems to be prodding you to step out of your comfort zone

(maybe by leaving home, or taking on new levels of responsibility like marriage or parenthood or a promotion, or sharing the gospel with someone), Jesus tells you to trust him (Proverbs 3 v 5-6). Wherever you go, his goodness and love will be pursuing you, so you can let go of the worries that hold you back. True security is found in boldly following Jesus, not in making risk-averse choices to stick to familiar and comfortable places. Obeying him is harder, but it's better.

Is the Lord Jesus is calling you to follow him in a particular way, but you're reluctant because it sounds too hard? Actually, let me rephrase that: how is the Lord Jesus right now calling you to follow him in a particular way, but you're reluctant because it sounds too hard? Remember that the best path is often the steeper one. Green pastures often lie beyond a rocky climb. When Jesus leads you along a way you would not have chosen and do not find easy, remember: he is your shepherd. And he's very, very good at it.

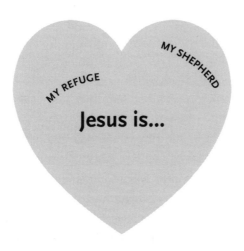

6. Light

"The LORD is my light."
Psalm 27 v 1

When I was young, my bedroom was terrifying at night. When it was dark, intruders hid in the shadows. Monsters lurked under the bed. If I made any noise, or if any part of my body protruded from the covers, they would get me.

There are dark corners in our city where I don't like walking at night. When I can't see what (or who) is ahead of me, my heart beats faster and my palms sweat. Every muscle becomes tensed, and the smallest noise makes me jump. My overactive imagination fills the unseen blackness with silent assassins, ready to pounce.

Darkness is a place of fear. Horror films rarely take place in broad daylight. It's difficult to be confident when you can't see.

When I was young, my parents put a night-light in my bedroom. With that, I was brave enough to relax and go to sleep. Light is a great giver of courage. When I walk through our city, I walk more confidently where there are streetlights.

So we instinctively understand the image David is using

when he describes the Lord as his light. He is saying: *Here is my source of courage and confidence.*

> "The LORD is my light and my salvation—
>   whom shall I fear?
> The LORD is the stronghold of my life—
>   of whom shall I be afraid?
> When the wicked advance against me
>   to devour me,
> it is my enemies and my foes
>   who will stumble and fall.
> Though an army besiege me,
>   my heart will not fear;
> though war break out against me,
>   even then I will be confident." (Psalm 27 v 1-3)

The Bible uses the image of light in two main ways. First, light is the source of life (e.g. Psalm 56 v 10-13)—almost all life on our planet is dependent on the sun. So Jesus is the light of the world because he is the source of eternal life (John 8 v 12). Second, light is the source of truth (e.g. Psalm 119 v 105, 130)—by the light of the sun we see the world around us, so that we're not left "in the dark". So Jesus is the light of the world because he reveals God to us, as the radiance of the sun reveals the sun to us (John 9 v 5).

Having the Lord Jesus as our light means that we look to him as our source of both life and truth. His light enables us to live with confidence and courage.

Choose your light
All of us choose a light—someone to give us the courage to walk through life. If we don't look to Jesus, we will look to other people to tell us what is true and to give us our confidence.

David was the same. "Whom shall I fear?" he asks in Psalm 27 v 1. This is crucial for us, because so much of our escapism is driven by a fear of what people think of us—by living in awe of their glory.

We put off decisions because we're trying to second-guess what other people want us to do.

We say yes to an invitation when we have no intention of going, because we don't like to disappoint people to their face.

We fail to invite anyone into our home for a meal because they might think our cooking or cleaning is not up to scratch.

We banter with our friends or stick to talking about sport or the kids, rather than being serious or vulnerable, because we don't want to seem weak or dull.

As Christians, we are tongue-tied and scared to tell friends the great news about Jesus because it might offend them (which is code for, it might mean they don't like or respect us).

Pastors don't challenge the deadly sins that their congregation cherish, because their congregation will be annoyed.

It's easy to see that thinking too lowly of other people stops us loving them. But thinking too highly of other people also stops us loving them. It makes us manipulate our friends and family instead of speaking openly to them. It holds us back from initiating conversation or friendship, or romance or sex, because we will be devastated by rejection. It leads us to spoil our children because we feel a need for their approval.

This is how psychologist Edward T. Welch puts it in his book *When People are Big and God is Small*:

> "Regarding other people, our problem is that we need them (for ourselves) more than we love them (for the glory of God). The task God sets for us is to need them less and love them more."

When people become your light, you fear them and you need them, but you do not love them. They become your source of life, making you desperate for their approval and any honour they might bestow. And they become your source of truth, so that their words and desires direct your actions. So instead of speaking the truth, we say what is palatable. Instead of doing what is right, we do what is popular. Peer pressure doesn't stop when we grow up.

That's one of the reasons why Jesus said that "Love your neighbour" is the second commandment. Only when we love the Lord our God with an undivided heart are we free to love our neighbour rather than needing them or fearing them. And the key is to see how Jesus is a brighter light than the people whose approval and guidance we seek. When you live in the light of the noonday sun, you don't need candles.

The brightest light

Why does David say that the Lord is his light? Psalm 27 continues:

"One thing I ask from the LORD,
   this only do I seek:
that I may dwell in the house of the LORD
   all the days of my life,
to gaze on the beauty of the LORD
   and to seek him in his temple.
For in the day of trouble
   he will keep me safe in his dwelling;
he will hide me in the shelter of his sacred tent
   and set me high upon a rock." (Psalm 27 v 4-5)

David speaks with an undivided heart—he asks for just "one thing". All he wants is to dwell with God and to gaze on his beauty. David finds the Lord more attractive than any human being. No one else compares to the Lord in beauty. No one else is as kind or as reliable or as generous or as majestic or as pure or as committed or as courageous as the Lord is. Whoever else David might desire, God is better.

Not only is he better, he is also greater. Armies might advance against David and enemies might besiege him, but God will keep him safe. No one else compares to Jesus in strength. No one else can calm storms or tame demons or defeat evil or rise from the dead. Whoever else David might fear, God is bigger.

We find this same combination—that the Lord is bigger and better than anyone else—in other places where the Bible urges us to be courageous and confident. It shouldn't surprise us that as Jesus sent his first followers out on their first mission trip, this was his theme:

> "Do not be afraid of those who kill the body but cannot kill the soul. Rather, be afraid of the One who can destroy both soul and body in hell. Are not two sparrows sold for a penny? Yet not one of them will fall to the ground outside your Father's care. And even the very hairs of your head are all numbered. So don't be afraid; you are worth more than many sparrows."
>
> (Matthew 10 v 28-31)

What a striking pair of pictures Jesus sets alongside each other! In one verse, God is a fierce and fearsome Judge; in the next, he's a gentle and generous Father. He can destroy more of me than people can, but he also protects more of me than people can. He's both bigger and better. What difference does knowing this make? "Do not be afraid."

If we want to be free from worrying about what other

people think of us, we need both these pictures. We need to know our Father is bigger than people, because that frees us from fearing them. We fret about whether people might blank us, or gossip about us, or body-shame us, or write a bad appraisal, or think we're bad parents when our kids throw a tantrum in public. But what's the worst they can do? They can only kill our body—but God "can destroy both soul and body in hell". The consequences of not pleasing God are far worse than those of not appeasing a human being.

And we need to know our Father is better than people, because that frees us from needing them. We need our manager's approval to keep or improve our job; we need our friends' approval to keep us from loneliness; we need our parents' approval in case we run out of money. But God's care for us goes way beyond the care we might receive from our company, our friends, or even our human parents. He loves us as our Father. He's counted the hairs on your head, the wrinkles on your brow, the aches in your joints and the scars in your heart. You don't need anyone else but him.

After all, whoever you are intimidated by, it's very unlikely you have it as hard as the first-century church in Pergamum, a generation after Jesus died, rose, and returned to heaven. The first imperial temple in Asia was built in this city, and one of the Christians there had recently been killed for not joining in with worshipping the emperor. They had good reason to fear the people around them! But look at how Jesus addresses them:

> "These are the words of him who has the sharp, double-edged sword. I know where you live—where Satan has his throne. Yet you remain true to my name. You did not renounce your faith in me, not even in the days of

Antipas, my faithful witness, who was put to death in your city—where Satan lives.

"Nevertheless, I have a few things against you: there are some among you who hold to the teaching of Balaam, who taught Balak to entice the Israelites to sin so that they ate food sacrificed to idols and committed sexual immorality. Likewise, you also have those who hold to the teaching of the Nicolaitans. Repent therefore! Otherwise, I will soon come to you and will fight against them with the sword of my mouth."

(Revelation 2 v 12-16)

Jesus wants this church to know that he is bigger and stronger than the local army and executioner. Jesus' sword is "sharp"—it cuts deep. And Jesus' sword is "double-edged"—it both protects and judges. He's more than a match for the Romans.

In the film *Crocodile Dundee*, there's a scene where Dundee and Sue are held up as they're leaving a restaurant. A gang of youths demand Dundee's wallet. Sue urges him to hand it over because one of them has a flick-knife.

"That's not a knife," says Dundee, pulling out his huge hunting blade: "*That's* a knife".

That's what Jesus says to the church in Pergamum:

Jesus: Keep following me and serving me
Church: But the Romans are hammering us! And they have swords!
Jesus: That's not a sword. *This* is a sword.

The sword of Jesus' mouth is far sharper and more dangerous than the sword of the authorities. That's why in reality, the biggest threat to this church isn't what people might to do them, because Jesus is fighting on their side. The biggest threat is their sin, because if they continue to cherish sin, then they'll find Jesus fighting against them. They don't need to worry about the Romans and the executioner; they do need to worry about their lack of sexual integrity and their tolerance of teachers who distort the gospel. Jesus wields the sharpest sword.

But Jesus also reassures them that he is better than the Romans:

> "Whoever has ears, let them hear what the Spirit says to the churches. To the one who is victorious, I will give some of the hidden manna. I will also give that person a white stone with a new name written on it, known only to the one who receives it." (Revelation 2 v 17)

Jesus gives them three things. First, there's hidden manna— bread to keep going through the desert, just as God fed his people manna in the desert on their way to the land he had promised to give them (Exodus 16). These Christians might lose their jobs or be banned from the market because of their faith, but Jesus will supply them with the spiritual calories to keep following him when it's hard.

Second, Jesus gives them each a white stone. In ancient trials this was a sign that someone was justified and pronounced innocent. They might be convicted in a Roman court, but in God's court—the highest in the cosmos—they are acquitted, vindicated and freed.

Third, Jesus gives each of them a new name. They are adopted into his family. They might lose their reputation or even their loved ones for worshipping Jesus, but Jesus will give them an identity as God's child and membership in his worldwide, eternal family.

The Lord Jesus is bigger and better than anyone else we might fear or need.

Walking in the light

Living for the approval of other people is like walking home at night down a dark alley where the streetlights aren't working. It's like five-year-old me trying to sleep without a night-light. It's a life of fear.

And it's totally unnecessary. Jesus is the light of the world. When we walk in his daylight, we don't need flickering torches. We're free to love people instead of needing them or fearing them. The rest of Psalm 27 shows how.

First, we don't need people's honour. Often we fail to do what is good and loving because we want people to honour us and not to shame us. But David looks to the Lord to honour him:

"For in the day of trouble
   he will keep me safe in his dwelling;
he will hide me in the shelter of his sacred tent
   and set me high upon a rock.
Then my head will be exalted
   above the enemies who surround me;
at his sacred tent I will sacrifice with shouts of joy;
   I will sing and make music to the LORD."

(Psalm 27 v 5-6)

David knows that Jesus will set him high and exalt him. We can know that in the gospel, Jesus gives us honour far beyond anything we could enjoy in human society. We're raised up with him and seated with him at God's right hand in the heavenly realms (Ephesians 2 v 6-7). He shares with us his status as God's son and heir (Galatians 4 v 4-7). He gives us the dignity of being his brothers and sisters (Hebrews 2 v 11; Mark 3 v 35). He makes us into temples for his Holy Spirit to dwell in (1 Corinthians 6 v 19).

This frees us from needing any of the petty honours this world gives. You can turn up to church with your imperfect children without worrying whether anyone thinks you're a good parent. You can do the humiliating tasks that other people think are below their dignity. You can speak for Jesus without worrying whether you're thought of as cool or sophisticated or intelligent or progressive or respectable. You can enjoy worldly honour, but you don't need it. The Lord has exalted you!

Second, we don't need people's approval. Our escapism can be prompted by our need for people to accept us. There can be few of us who have never failed to challenge a friend's destructive behaviour. Why? Because at that moment we felt we needed friendship with them more than we wanted what was best for them. If you need someone's approval, you are never able to simply be yourself and you're never able to do what is best for them (unless it happens to be what will make them keep liking you). But David doesn't need people's approval—he knows that he enjoys the approval of someone who is stronger and more beautiful.

> "Hear my voice when I call, LORD;
>   be merciful to me and answer me.
> My heart says of you, "Seek his face!"
>   Your face, LORD, I will seek.
> Do not hide your face from me,
>   do not turn your servant away in anger;
>   you have been my helper.
> Do not reject me or forsake me,
>   God my Saviour.
> Though my father and mother forsake me,
>   the LORD will receive me." (Psalm 27 v 7-10)

We can't be sure that people will still receive us tomorrow (which is why pleasing them is so tiring), but we can be sure with the Lord. Even if something happened that caused his father and mother to reject him, David knew that God would still accept him. Wonderfully, we can be even more confident of this than King David was. On the cross, Jesus was deserted so that we will never be (Mark 15 v 34). God has promised never to leave us or forsake us (Hebrews 13 v 5-6). We are justified in Christ so that God looks on us with the same delight with which he looks on Jesus (Romans 5 v 1-2).

When you experience this as a reality in your heart, it frees you from needing the approval of people around you. Instead of needing them, you can love them. You can bear your children being angry with you when you say no to their demands. You can turn down the advances of the attractive non-Christian at work, because you know that staying unmarried and unattached doesn't mean you are unloved. The Lord will receive you!

I think one of the more tragic moments in the Bible comes as we watch a man fail to appreciate this. Pontius Pilate had an easy decision to make. As the Roman Governor of Judea, he had cross-examined Jesus and questioned Jesus' accusers, who were demanding his execution; and the conclusion was not hard to reach. Jesus had done nothing wrong. The verdict was obvious. Except that Pilate feared the approval of men. He wanted to satisfy the crowd. He didn't want the religious leaders to complain about him. He worried about what the emperor might do. Because Pilate lived for human approval and honour, this decision became hard. Too hard. He ducked doing what was just, and instead sent an innocent man to his death. As it happened, the innocent man who died because of Pilate's cowardice was the Son of God, his Judge.

Without the Lord as our light, it's impossible to do what is right. When we look to him for our confidence and courage, it's still not easy, but it is possible. Contrast the powerful Roman Pilate with two slave midwives in Egypt over a millennium before. Another emperor, the Pharaoh, had an immigration problem. To solve it, he demanded that the midwives murder any newborn boys born to the Hebrews. But they refused to bow to the king's vicious decree. Why? Because they "feared God" (Exodus 1 v 17). They knew that the Lord was bigger and better than the emperor. So they looked to the Lord to honour them.

Pharaoh would have been the most famous man on earth in his day. Today, no one knows his name. Yet God recorded the names of those midwives, Shiphrah and Puah, in his word, to be honoured for all time. With the Lord as our light, we can resist any pressure to do what is wrong.

Living with confidence

Which people are big in your thinking? Work out whose anger you fear, whose blessing you feel you need, and whose approval you dare not lose. When have you failed to do what you know is right because of who would see you? When have you kept quiet when you knew you ought to speak because of who would hear you? Whose reactions do you worry about when you have a decision to make? Whose opinions are most powerful in forming yours?

These people—whether they are friends or enemies, lovely or unlikeable—are the candles who threaten to take the place of Jesus' sun in your life.

Picture one of those people in your mind. And now picture them next to the crucified and risen Lord Jesus. Who is bigger? Who is better? Who is a more reliable source of truth and life? Who flickers like a candle and who shines like the sun? Now reflect on whose disapproval you fear, and whose approval you really need. Pray through Psalm 27, Matthew 10 and Revelation 2, asking the Holy Spirit to help you live in the light.

With the Lord Jesus as your light, you can have the same confidence and courage as David:

> "I remain confident of this:
>> I will see the goodness of the LORD
>> in the land of the living.
> Wait for the LORD;
>> be strong and take heart
>> and wait for the LORD." (Psalm 27 v 13-14)

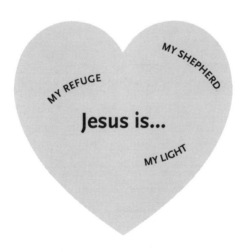

7. Portion

"The LORD is my portion."
Lamentations 3 v 24

Have you ever had a meal that was so small that you were still hungry at the end? Maybe it was because the cupboard was bare, or you were on a diet, or you went to a fashionable restaurant that charges big money for tiny meals? The meal was over, but you still wanted to raid the cookie jar—because you hadn't had your portion.

On the other hand, have you ever eaten so much that it made you feel sick? Perhaps it was an all-you-can-eat buffet you couldn't resist, or a gluttonous Christmas dinner, or a low-mood binge on chocolate and ice cream? Having more than your portion can feel just as bad as having less.

Compare those feelings with the joy of a full, but not too full, stomach at the end of a tasty meal with friends—a meal that was just the right size. No hunger, no bloated feeling, just contentment. That's the feeling of having your portion.

Whatever amount of food you need to be satisfied is your portion. Less than your portion, and you're still hungry; more than your portion, and you feel sick; but with your portion, you're content.

That's the feeling that's being described when people in the Bible say that God is their portion. They're saying that God is their three-course meal. Without God, they're still hungry; with him, they don't need anything else to be content, and so trying to have other things in addition to him makes them less happy, not more.

They're not always talking about food when they say that God is their portion. The word "portion" also describes a plot of land that someone inherits. So when Joshua and the Israelites enter the promised land, Joshua "apportions" to each family their own property. This God-given turf gives that family its identity, its food and its security for the future.

So the Christian can say, "The LORD is my portion". Without him, we can't be satisfied; with him, we don't need anything or anyone else to be content. At least, that's the theory. But how can it be reality?

The fear of missing out

Contentment is a rare jewel. It probably always was, but it is especially so now because of the explosion of choice. Our ancestors had very few choices: they would live where they grew up, take up their father's trade or their mother's place in the home, eat what they could grow and wear what they could make. But now my local 24-hour supermarket is the size of a football pitch, and I can choose between dozens of TVs, toilet tissues and tins of tuna. On the internet, the choice is even wider. I now have to choose where to live, what styles to wear, what job to do, what music to listen to and what destinations to travel to.

The result is that we're always aware of the other choices

we could have made—and of the choices that other people are making. If I go to this concert, I can't go to that exhibition. If I live in this city, I can't live on that coast. If I buy this phone, I can't afford those shoes. I'm aware of the opportunity cost of every decision. This results in FOMO: the Fear Of Missing Out. The Oxford Dictionary defines it as:

> "Anxiety that an exciting or interesting event may
> currently be happening elsewhere, often aroused by
> posts seen on social media."

This fear of missing out lies behind a lot of escapism. A friend cancels coffee because a better offer came up. A Christian with same-sex attraction finds celibacy hard when they see another happy gay couple on TV. A retired lady resents caring for her grandchildren when her friends on Facebook are travelling the world ticking off items on their bucket lists. A girl on a night out barely talks to anyone because she's scanning her friends' Snapchat stories to see what else she could have been doing.

But it's not just a fear of missing out on what we could have—it's also a fear of losing the comforts we do have. Call it FOLO—fear of losing out. A young man never calls his grandmother because it can't compete with the adrenaline rush of playing Call of Duty. Churches shrink and die because members won't make the changes needed to make the gospel accessible to new generations. We pretty much all know that our lifestyles are causing uncontrollable climate change, but we can't bear the thought of cutting back on our air miles, car travel or electricity use.

Adverts feed FOMO and FOLO. They are designed to make us discontent until we've bought the product on offer. The media show the rich and famous doing exciting things that we'd love to do too. Western capitalism could barely function without this envy. And we feed ourselves too. We are doing it whenever we plaster Instagram with a highlights reel of our day, implying that we never have to change nappies, check emails or do the washing up. We used to show our holiday photos to people who knew us well and who saw the downs as well as the ups—now on Facebook we display the ups to those who never see the downs. Social media has rightly been called a petri dish for envy.

So if we want to choose what is best rather than what is easiest, we need to learn the secret of being content. And to do that, we need to discover how God can be our portion. Only when God is our three-course meal, will we be able to turn down the scraps of box sets and the junk food of self-indulgent travel. Only when we find all our happiness in Jesus will we be liberated to let go of our other comforts.

We are God's portion

The prophet Jeremiah preached to people who looked for happiness from somewhere other than God—in their idols and possessions. In calling God's people ("Jacob") back to the Lord, he reminded them that God was their portion—and that they were God's portion.

"He who is the Portion of Jacob is not like these [idols],
   for he is the Maker of all things,
including Israel, the people of his inheritance—
   the LORD Almighty is his name." (Jeremiah 10 v 16)

Jeremiah says that God treasures us as his inheritance— his portion. Amazingly, what gives God pleasure is his relationship with his people. What God is looking forward to is gathering his people around him as his family in the new creation. We are God's portion, and he delights in us.

We find the same idea elsewhere in the Bible:

> "I pray that the eyes of your heart may be enlightened
> in order that you may know the hope to which he has
> called you, the riches of his glorious inheritance in his
> holy people, and his incomparably great power for us
> who believe." (Ephesians 1 v 18-19)

God can't wait for the day when he makes us all as glorious as Jesus is and lives with us for ever. We are God's portion, which means that we are precious to God, and that he takes pleasure in us.

The nineteenth-century poet and art critic John Ruskin once wrote, "The best things in life are not things". We all know that the greatest joys in life come from relationships—from being loved and cherished. So what greater joy can there be than being loved and cherished by the God who made the universe, the Lord Almighty, the Father of our Lord Jesus Christ? God is our treasure and our portion, because we are God's treasure and God's portion.

God is our portion for ever

David wrote Psalm 16 when he was full of delight in God:

> "LORD, you alone are my portion and my cup;
> you make my lot secure." (Psalm 16 v 5)

The Lord is his source of happiness. And what makes David smile is what God has stored up for him in the future:

> "Therefore my heart is glad and my tongue rejoices;
> my body also will rest secure,
> because you will not abandon me to the realm of the dead,
> nor will you let your faithful one see decay.

You make known to me the path of life;
    you will fill me with joy in your presence,
    with eternal pleasures at your right hand."

(Psalm 16 v 9-11)

We're used to experiencing present happiness because of a future event. The thought of the end of term helps us to endure double maths. The expectation of holding her baby sustains a mother during a difficult pregnancy. The hope of remission gets a cancer patient through the pain of chemotherapy.

David rejoices in the present because of what God will do for him in the future. God won't let his body decay in the grave; he will be resurrected. That resurrection life will be fantastic because it will be lived in God's presence—his joy will be full and his pleasures will be eternal.

David is sure that as he lives with faith in his God, his God will take him through death. And we can be sure of that too, because this psalm looks forward to another king: the faithful one, who was not abandoned in "the realm of the dead". King Jesus' resurrection is the proof that God has defeated death for his people (see Acts 2 v 24-32). Everyone who trusts in Jesus is united to him so that we will share in his resurrection (see Romans 8 v 11). That means that we have the same hope that David had.

Your joys will be full

In eternity, God promises to fill us with joy. He guarantees us maximum satisfaction—happiness turned up to 11. He can do that because he made us for a relationship with himself, so in that relationship we will be truly complete. And he can do that because he is an infinitely gracious, creative God who will never tire of dreaming up new ways to be kind and generous to us:

> "And God raised us up with Christ and seated us with
> him in the heavenly realms in Christ Jesus, in order that
> in the coming ages he might show the incomparable
> riches of his grace, expressed in his kindness to us in
> Christ Jesus." (Ephesians 2 v 6-7)

With this future guaranteed, you don't actually need anything else to be content now. You don't need material riches (which so often and easily isolate us from other people) when you are satisfied with the incomparable riches of God's grace. You don't need self-centred me-time when you have so much time with Jesus to look forward to. You don't need to live in an attractive or safe location now when you will live in such a divine location in eternity. You don't need to spoil your appetite by snacking on this junk food when a banquet is waiting for you.

Your pleasures will be eternal

Jesus warns people not to waste time chasing after pleasures that do not last.

> "Do not work for food that spoils, but for food that
> endures to eternal life, which the Son of Man will give
> you ... I am the bread of life. Whoever comes to me will
> never go hungry, and whoever believes in me will never
> be thirsty." (John 6 v 27, 35)

Jesus wants to free us from craving the short-term pleasures of an easy life now by feeding us with the eternal pleasure of knowing him. When you're hungry, even disgusting food can look appetising. But when you're full, you can turn down even tasty food.

So you can say no to the short-term escape of porn or an erotic novel when you remember Jesus' promise that you will never go hungry. You can commit to celibacy or one spouse for life now when you consider that you will miss out on nothing in eternity. You can accept the unpleasant jobs that ruin your comfort now when your eyes are fixed on the eternal pleasures at God's right hand. You don't need to complete a "bucket list" now when you'll have eternity to explore the new creation. You may never visit the Niagara Falls before you die—but you'll have for ever to enjoy it—or a wonder even greater—with Jesus.

God is our portion *now*

Let's face it, though, knowing that we'll be happy with God in eternity doesn't always help us when we're unhappy today. As Proverbs 13 v 12 says, "Hope deferred makes a heart sick". Or as a friend of mine who struggles with comfort eating puts it, "I know it's going to be great in heaven, but in the meantime I'll have chocolate". What he and you and I all need to grasp is that God is also our portion now. He is our jam today as well as tomorrow.

Psalm 73 was written by a man with a severe case of FOMO. Asaph worshipped God, but when he looked around at all the fun his unbelieving friends were having, he wanted to throw in the towel:

"Surely God is good to Israel,
   to those who are pure in heart.
But as for me, my feet had almost slipped;
   I had nearly lost my foothold.
For I envied the arrogant
   when I saw the prosperity of the wicked."

(Psalm 73 v 1-3)

Asaph looked around at everyone else's big houses and holiday snaps and shiny new watches, and felt he was missing out. He envied people who weren't living for God, and who seemed so much happier than him. All that effort staying pure and serving others and working for justice was a waste of time:

"This is what the wicked are like—

always free of care, they go on amassing wealth.

Surely in vain I have kept my heart pure

and have washed my hands in innocence.

All day long I have been afflicted,

and every morning brings new punishments." (v 12-14)

But then he enters God's sanctuary, and he remembers two truths that change his perspective. First, he remembers the ultimate fate of people who reject God—that God will reject them (v 15-20). Second, he remembers God's goodness to him and how wonderful it is to know God:

"Yet I am always with you;

you hold me by my right hand.

You guide me with your counsel,

and afterwards you will take me into glory.

Whom have I in heaven but you?

And earth has nothing I desire besides you.

My flesh and my heart may fail,

but God is the strength of my heart

and my portion for ever." (v 23-26)

At the end of the psalm, Asaph is a great model of enjoying God as our portion now, as well as for ever. He has an undivided heart that only desires God. He couldn't be content without God; but with God he needs nothing else to be happy. When his friends are enjoying the high life, he doesn't envy them because he feels like he's just eaten a three-course meal.

It's one thing to see that Asaph viewed life like this. It's a very different thing to do so ourselves. We need to remember and reflect on three joys that Asaph picks out that make God a satisfying portion now:

First, there is God's grip. "You hold me by my right hand" (v 23): when we feel alone, God is with us by his Spirit; when we are confused, he leads us; when we are slipping, he holds us; when we fall, he lifts us to our feet; when we are losing our grip on him, he tightens his grip on us.

Second, there is God's guidance. "You guide me with your counsel" (v 24): God speaks to us through his word; he leads us to the promised land by his Spirit; he strengthens us by his promises; he teaches us wisdom and helps us to make good choices.

Third, there is God's glory. "You will take me into glory" (v 24): the destination will make even the hard parts of the journey worthwhile—we will see and share Jesus' divine majesty (2 Peter 1 v 4). We will live in a world where God's presence has banished death and crying and pain (Revelation 21 v 1-4).

Pictures of contentment

Caleb is honoured in the Bible as a man who followed the Lord with an undivided heart (Joshua 14 v 14). When he discovered that the promised land was full of fortified cities and strong warriors, he rose to the challenge (Numbers 13 v 26-30). When all but one of his fellow Israelites advised caution and retreat (and threatened to stone him), Caleb stood firm in publicly trusting God (Numbers 14 v 1-10). Not for Caleb an easy retirement by the coast; at the age of 85, he was still leading the charge against the fearsome Anakites (Joshua 14 v 10-12).

What sustained this lifelong courage and willingness to take risks for God? The promise of an inheritance, a portion:

> "So on that day Moses swore to me, 'The land on which your feet have walked will be your inheritance and that of your children for ever, because you have followed the LORD my God wholeheartedly'." (Joshua 14 v 9)

> "In accordance with the LORD's command to him, Joshua gave to Caleb son of Jephunneh a portion in Judah—Kiriath Arba, that is, Hebron." (Joshua 15 v 13)

Courage and commitment come from contentment. Wholeheartedness flows from a heart that doesn't worry about whether it is missing out. What might Caleb look like in the ups and downs of daily 21st-century life?

Arjun has noticed (and has been told by his wife) that his phone is taking over his life. When he has the kids, he puts the TV on for them and plays on his phone. When he's with people he doesn't know, he turns to his phone. When he's with people he does know and the conversation dips, he picks up his phone. The lure of a "computer cuddle" is more instantly rewarding than whiny kids or stilted conversation, even if in the long term it makes his relationships distant and unfulfilling.

But Arjun is convicted that he has been doing what is easiest for himself, not what is best for those around him. And in his daily Bible-reading (which he no longer does on his phone) he's discovered and memorised Psalm 73 v 25-26. So now he doesn't need his phone to make him happy. He's deleted his email app and turned off the alerts, and tries to only look at his phone at set times of day when he's on his own. He's seeking to be present and engaged with the people around him, however awkward that sometimes feels. It's getting easier. And he feels... well, satisfied.

Joan loves her church, and feels very comfortable there. She knows all the hymns and all the people. But numbers are dwindling, and very few of the next generation are attending. She loves Jesus and wants him to be honoured in everyone's life, but her desire for comfort is getting in the way.

Joan finds change unsettling, but she knows that if church is always done the way she likes it, many people of a younger generation or a different cultural background will never get to know Jesus. As she chats with other core members at church, they resolve to change their attitude. They will come to church to serve, not consume. They will rejoice when they sing new songs, and not grumble. They will welcome people who are different to them, instead of just talking with old friends. And when it's hard (and it is hard), they remind each other that their happiness doesn't come from comfortable Sundays at church, but from having a wonderful hope, being infinitely precious to God, and knowing his power is at work for them. It's getting to feel more natural. And she feels... well, happier.

Liam and Kate have high-earning jobs. They can afford a house in an affluent area with good schools, while still travelling abroad and eating out each week. But they are aware that wealth tends to isolate them from other people and their struggles, and to elevate them above other people too. And because they are looking forward to the new creation, where their joy will be full and their pleasures eternal, they don't need those things. Accumulating more stuff just makes them feel as if they've got indigestion.

So Liam and Kate choose to live in a rough area that has many problems and few Christians. Liam works part-time so he can volunteer at church and start up a local social enterprise. They use their house for hospitality, and the smaller mortgage means they can give nearly half their incomes away each year to church and other charities—because the Lord is their portion. Their bank account is far emptier. But they feel... well, fuller.

And then there's *you*. Are you enjoying the Lord as your portion? Can you say with confidence that Jesus is all you need to be content? Do you feel hungry and desperate for more, because you're looking elsewhere instead of to Jesus? Or maybe you feel busy and bloated because you're looking elsewhere in addition to him?

Reflect on where you're looking for happiness. When you put off an unpleasant job, identify what you turn to instead. What comforts do you cling to that keep you from loving other people? What couldn't you bear to live without? What are you afraid you might be missing out on?

Now compare those joys with the wonder of knowing Jesus. Can they satisfy you as much as having a relationship with the God who made you? Are they foods that endure to eternal life, or foods that spoil? Work out what you need to give up or give away in order to remove that bloated feeling.

In that moment when you are tempted to not love others because you are afraid you will miss out, remember that the choice is between a healthy and filling three-course meal or a scrap of junk food. Nothing else and no one else offers you the grip, the guidance, and the glory of the Lord Jesus. An undivided heart enjoys him as its portion.

MY REFUGE

MY SHEPHERD

Jesus is...

MY PORTION

MY LIGHT

8. Rock

"The LORD is my rock."
Psalm 18 v 2

Where will you stand when the storm strikes?

On 28th November 1905, the Mataafa Storm swept through the Great Lakes, damaging 29 ships and killing 36 seamen. One ship, the *Madeira*, grounded at the bottom of some cliffs. As the waves pounded the boat, it began to break up.

Grasping a rope, Fred Benson, one of the crew, leaped from the deck to the cliff, and climbed 60 feet to the top of those cliffs—to a place called Gold Rock. From there, he dropped the line down to the boat, and eight crewmates climbed up to him. Standing on Gold Rock, they endured the storm, safe from the waves and breakers below. Two days later they were picked up and returned home.

There are times in life when the storms rage and our troubles threaten to sweep us away. In those moments we need somewhere to stand that lifts us above the waves. We need something firm to hold onto. We need a rock—a rock strong enough to bear our weight.

I don't know the details of your life, but I do know that either you are in a storm right now, or that one day you will be. So—what rock will you stand on when the tempest rages?

Immovable Rock

At the end of his life, Moses wrote a song about God to encourage God's people to keep trusting the Lord after his death. The dominant image of the song is that God is the Rock (Deuteronomy 32 v 4, 15, 18, 30, 31).

Moses wants to describe how immovable and dependable this Rock is, and he has to stretch the limits of language and grammar to do it. In Hebrew, he manages to describe God the Rock without using any verbs. Here's my attempt to translate it into English:

> "The Rock: His works—perfect; all his ways—just;
> A God of faithfulness and without injustice;
> Righteous and upright." (Deuteronomy 32 v 4)

Perfect, just, faithful, good, righteous and upright—and not a single verb in sight. There isn't even an "is"! I think that's because a verb has a tense, which would restrict God to the past, the present or the future. And Moses wants people to grasp that God is the Rock in the past, the present and the future. Plus, a verb implies movement. And Moses wants to communicate how unchangeable and constant God is. So he sticks to nouns and adjectives. Our steady and dependable Rock. Old Testament scholar James Robson puts it this way:

> "There is not a single finite verb or participle. There is no action, no movement; only realities. Rocks do not change—they are permanent."
>
> (*Honey from the Rock*, pages 56-57)

A rock is battered by a storm and it does not bend. The waves beat against it but it does not fall. Our weight presses down on it but it does not sink. That is our God: always perfect; always just; always faithful, righteous and upright; never unjust. So you can trust him and cling to him today, tomorrow and every day.

> "Trust in the LORD for ever,
>   for the LORD, the LORD himself, is the Rock
>   eternal." (Isaiah 26 v 4)

Isn't that just what you need when it feels as if the bottom has fallen out of your world? You need a firm place to stand and a firm handhold to grip. You need this when you're bereaved, when your partner walks out on you or when you find a lump on your breast or your testicle.

When everything else is uncertain, God is sure.

When everyone else lets you down, God is faithful.

When everything around you is in flux, God will not change.

He is the Rock.

This is what Joseph, of the famous "technicolour dreamcoat", discovered in his sufferings. His father Jacob described it like this:

> "With bitterness archers attacked [Joseph];
>   they shot at him with hostility.
> But his bow remained steady,
>   his strong arms stayed supple,
> because of the hand of the Mighty One of Jacob,
>   because of the Shepherd, the Rock of Israel,
> because of your father's God, who helps you,
>   because of the Almighty, who blesses you."
>
>   (Genesis 49 v 23-25)

Joseph was envied by his brothers and sold as a slave for twenty shekels of silver. He was trafficked to Egypt and forced to work for a man named Potiphar. He was falsely accused of sexual assault and locked in a dungeon. He was forgotten by the friend who had promised to help him.

Yet through all this, God was with Joseph. God helped him to work well as a slave. God blessed him so that he was put in charge of the prison. God raised him up to become Pharaoh's right-hand man in charge of keeping Egypt alive through a seven-year famine. God was Joseph's Rock in his lowest moments.

We see the same pattern in Jesus' life. He too was betrayed, sold for silver and falsely accused. He too trusted God as his Rock, and placed himself in God's hands (see Luke 23 v 46, quoting from Psalm 31 v 1-5). And he has been raised up to God's right hand in charge of God's global life-giving plan.

So Joseph would say to us what he said to his brothers:

"Don't be afraid. Am I in the place of God? You
intended to harm me, but God intended it for good
to accomplish what is now being done, the saving of
many lives. So then, don't be afraid."

(Genesis 50 v 19-21)

God has a wonderful way of taking what is evil and using it for good. We see it in Joseph, and we see it at the cross. In the evil, he helps us; and through the evil, he blesses us. He promises to use all the evil that you suffer for your ultimate good too (Romans 8 v 28). Your God, who walked this earth as Jesus Christ, is the immovable Rock—he has not changed:

"Jesus Christ is the same yesterday and today and for
ever." (Hebrews 13 v 8)

Incomparable Rock

Moses' song goes on to warn how God's people will be tempted to let go of their Rock to trust in idols. But Moses is adamant—idols are no substitute for the true God:

"For their rock is not like our Rock,
as even our enemies concede." (Deuteronomy 32 v 31)

No one can compare with our Rock.

Hannah discovered that in her grief. She was married to a bigamous husband. His other wife had children, "but Hannah had none" (1 Samuel 1 v 2). As for so many people today, infertility was a source of deep pain for Hannah, and it was made even worse by her husband's other wife provoking her, pushing her over the edge so she would break down in tears (1 Samuel 1 v 7).

But Hannah knew that God was her Rock. She turned to him in her misery, "weeping bitterly" as she prayed to him out of "deep anguish" (1 Samuel 1 v 10). When Eli the priest misunderstood her and thought she was drunk, she explained:

"I am a woman who is deeply troubled. I have not been drinking wine or beer; I was pouring out my soul to the LORD. Do not take your servant for a wicked woman; I have been praying here out of my great anguish and grief." (1 Samuel 1 v 15-16)

The Lord heard Hannah's prayer and remembered her, and gave her a son, Samuel. Hannah responded by doing something that was perhaps as difficult as enduring childlessness—she gave her only child to the Lord to serve him at the temple. She could do this because she knew that God was her incomparable Rock:

"There is no one holy like the LORD;

  there is no one besides you;

  there is no Rock like our God.

Do not keep talking so proudly

  or let your mouth speak such arrogance,

for the LORD is a God who knows,

  and by him deeds are weighed.

The bows of warriors are broken,

  but those who stumbled are armed with strength.

Those who were full hire themselves out for food,

  but those who were hungry are hungry no more.

She who was barren has borne seven children,

  but she who has had many sons pines away."

(1 Samuel 2 v 2-5)

What stuns Hannah is God's justice and his delight in reversing our situations and expectations. The strong are broken and the weak are strengthened; the full are famished and the hungry are filled; the barren woman has a full nursery and the gloating mother is left alone.

We see this same reversal in the gospel. Through Jesus, God showers his grace on the poor, but the rich cannot earn or buy his favour. God satisfies the hungry, but the well-fed are left wanting. God turns our weeping into laughter, but the joke's on those who laugh. God loves and welcomes those who are hated because they follow Jesus, but the popular are left out (read through Jesus' teaching in Luke 6 v 20-26). "For all those who exalt themselves will be humbled, and those who humble themselves will be exalted" (Luke 18 v 14).

That means that when we are at our lowest ebb, we can count on God. When we are most aware of our need, we are in the place where God loves to shower his blessings. No other god is gracious like our God. No other Rock can lift us up in the same way when the torrent of life knocks us down. We may not receive our answer in this life like Hannah did, but we can pour out our hearts to the Lord like she did, confident that there is no one like him.

Invincible Rock

King David had a long line of enemies trying to bring him down: vicious Goliath, the Philistine champion; jealous King Saul, who repeatedly tried to murder him; treacherous Doeg the Edomite, who killed hundreds of his friends; the Amalekites, who kidnapped his and his men's wives; his son Absalom, who conspired against him.

But David was resilient in the face of all these threats. He could keep on keeping on because he knew that God was his Rock:

> "Praise be to the LORD my Rock,
>   who trains my hands for war,
>   my fingers for battle.
> He is my loving God and my fortress,
>   my stronghold and my deliverer,
> my shield, in whom I take refuge,
>   who subdues peoples under me.
> LORD, what are human beings that you care for them,
>   mere mortals that you think of them?
> They are like a breath;
>   their days are like a fleeting shadow." (Psalm 144 v 1-4)

David was faithfully serving the LORD, so he knew that he was on the LORD's side. In all his struggles, he had the Rock on his team (or rather, he was on the Rock's team). He also knew that the people who were causing him hassle were like a breath, a mere shadow. A fight between the Rock and a breath has only one winner.

Jesus used this image of an unbeatable, immovable stone when he was warning his enemies not to keep fighting against him.

> "Jesus said to them, 'Have you never read in the Scriptures:
>
> > "The stone the builders rejected
> > has become the cornerstone;
> > the Lord has done this,
> > and it is marvellous in our eyes"?
>
> 'Therefore I tell you that the kingdom of God will be taken away from you and given to a people who will produce its fruit. Anyone who falls on this stone will be broken to pieces; anyone on whom it falls will be crushed.'" (Matthew 21 v 42-44)

Jesus knows that the Jewish leaders are going to reject him and hand him over to be crucified. But he also knows that he is an invincible Rock. God will raise him up and make him the cornerstone of God's new temple, the church—the one upon whom the only building that will last for ever will be constructed. Human hostility cannot defeat Jesus. Even death is no match for him. Our Messiah will "crush" his opponents until they are "broken to pieces". He is our invincible Rock.

So whoever is opposing you as you try to serve Jesus, don't give up. They are a breath; he is a Rock. There is only one winner. Whatever they say about you and do to you, Jesus will reverse it when he raises you up to reign with him in his new creation.

Inexhaustible Rock

God had called Israel out of slavery in Egypt and into the desert. Yet the desert journey was so tough that they began to miss the familiarity (and food) of captivity. How would God give them the resilience to keep on keeping on?

"The LORD answered Moses, 'Go out in front of the people. Take with you some of the elders of Israel and take in your hand the staff with which you struck the Nile, and go. I will stand there before you by the rock at Horeb. Strike the rock, and water will come out of it for the people to drink.' So Moses did this is the sight of the elders of Israel." (Exodus 17 v 5-6)

When it was struck by the staff of God's justice, the rock in the desert quenched Israel's thirst and sustained their faith for the journey. When we feel like we can't go on, we need an inexhaustible rock to drink from.

That rock is the Lord Jesus:

"[The people of Israel] all ate the same spiritual food and drank the same spiritual drink; for they drank from the spiritual rock that accompanied them, and that rock was Christ." (1 Corinthians 10 v 3-4)

And the water that Jesus gives us is his Holy Spirit:

"On the last and greatest day of the festival, Jesus stood and said in a loud voice, 'Let anyone who is thirsty come to me and drink. Whoever believes in me, as Scripture has said, rivers of living water will flow from within them.' By this he meant the Spirit, whom those who believed in him were later to receive. Up to that time the Spirit had not been given, since Jesus had not yet been glorified." (John 7 v 37-39)

However tough it is to keep going through suffering, and however hard it is to keep obeying God, you have an inexhaustible Rock. When Jesus died on the cross (when he was, to use John's language in those verses, "glorified"), he was struck with the staff of God's justice, so that his Spirit could be poured out into your heart. He was overwhelmed by the waters so that you never would be.

When you think you have reached the end of your reserves and that giving up is your only option, this is great news. You can come to Jesus and he will give you his Spirit to drink. He will make you resilient. He will give you the strength to take the next step.

Standing on the Rock

Bob Gough was a blind man at my last church. He used to be very active, but by the time I knew him he rarely left his bungalow. He had depression and anxiety, and felt that everyone was talking about him. He was in the storm.

I used to phone Bob most Fridays to ask him if he felt up to having a visitor. When he let me come round, I would encourage him to listen to his doctor and I would read a psalm to him. Bob found great solace in discovering that the believers who wrote the psalms had sometimes felt the way he did. One favourite was Psalm 42, where one of the sons of Korah is so depressed he can't eat, and feels as if he's sinking beneath the waves and that God has deserted him. Yet he also calls God "my Rock", and tells himself to keep putting his hope in God. So Bob would listen to a CD of psalms and Christian songs, to help himself to keep talking to God, his immovable Rock, when he felt as though God had packed up and moved out of his life.

Maybe, like Bob, you are being battered by one of life's

tornadoes. Maybe your mental or physical health is falling apart. Maybe you face racist bullying at school or sexist bullying at work. Maybe your benefits have been sanctioned or your business has failed. Maybe you've lost your savings in a scam or your possessions in a literal flood. Maybe it's something else that threatens to knock you off your feet.

Whatever storm you face, the Lord Jesus remains your immovable and inexhaustible Rock. He will supply you with his Spirit when you feel that you can't go on any more. So you don't need to escape. A girl who discovers she's pregnant and doesn't feel ready to be a mum can know that an abortion isn't the only way out. A woman grieving a miscarriage can look to Jesus for solace, and not to a bottle. A dad who can't see his kids can pray to Jesus for the Holy Spirit's help not to give in to despair and bitterness. A man who is coughing up blood can find the strength to see the doctor when he fears the worst.

Maybe it's not the storm today you struggle in, but the thought of a storm tomorrow. Are you holding back from a courageous decision because you worry that you might not be able to cope in a future storm? This is FOWI (a less catchy acronym)—Fear Of What Ifs. What if I'm made redundant? What if my friends let me down? What if I face persecution? What if I have to bring up this baby on my own? What if I get dementia? What if my doubts become stronger than my faith? What if it just turns out to be the wrong decision, and it's too late?

The truth that overcomes this fear is that even though you might not be able to cope, Jesus will be able to. However strong the storms, your Rock is stronger. However high the waves, your Rock lifts you higher. Your Rock is immovable, incomparable, invincible and inexhaustible. Your Rock will stand firm—so you have a firm place to stand. Stand on the Rock now, before the storm strikes, and the Rock will keep you standing firm when it does.

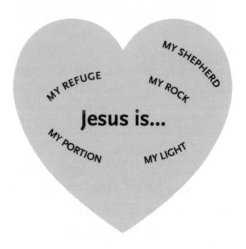

MY SHEPHERD

MY REFUGE

MY ROCK

Jesus is...

MY PORTION

MY LIGHT

9. Strength

"The LORD is my strength."
Exodus 15 v 2

"It won't work."

"I'd never be able to."

"I can't."

"I'm not the right person for this."

"It's too hard."

"We tried it before and it didn't work."

"I wouldn't be able to keep it up."

"I'd let people down."

"It won't make any difference."

These are just some of the excuses I store in my quiver to help me avoid difficult challenges. I persuade myself that if I'm no good at something, then there's no point trying. If it's not going to work anyway, then even starting would be a waste of time. I listen again to my life coach, Homer Simpson: "Trying is the first step towards failure". It's a self-fulfilling prophecy: *I can't, so I don't.* Perhaps I need a new life coach.

John Newton, for example. Newton, the ex-slave-trader who wrote the hymn "Amazing Grace", was a friend of William

Wilberforce, the Christian who campaigned for the British Parliament to abolish the slave trade. On 23rd February 1807, Wilberforce succeeded. It had taken twenty years. That he began such a campaign, against so many powerful vested interests, was a remarkable act of faith. That he kept rowing against the tide for two decades is even more astonishing. In 1796, he had nearly passed an Abolition Bill through Parliament, but lost by four votes (six of his supporters had gone to the opera instead). He became depressed and was ready to give up. This is how John Newton encouraged him to keep going:

> "It is true that you live in the midst of difficulties and snares, and you need a double guard of watchfulness and prayer. But since you know both of your need for help, and where to look for it, I may say to you as Darius to Daniel 'Thy God whom thou servest continually is able to preserve and deliver you.'"

Newton picks out two great reasons to attempt impossible things for Jesus: we know that God is able to help us, and we know that his strength comes to us not when we feel strong, but when we know our "need for help".

Whom the Lord strengthens

We keep falling for the lie that our weaknesses are obstacles to experiencing God's strength. So we don't mention Jesus to our friends because we think we wouldn't be able to answer their questions. We don't take on new responsibilities because we can't be sure we would be good at them. We don't bother to campaign against human trafficking or the arms trade or corporate tax evasion because we can't see how we could make any difference.

The message of the cross, however, is the opposite. Our strengths can be obstacles to having God's strength, because they can lead us to rely on ourselves and not pray; but our weaknesses are advantages, not hindrances, because they force us to rely on God and not on ourselves. We can see this by looking at what sort of people the Lord strengthens.

Strength for the weak

This is what the apostle Paul discovered about how to be filled with Jesus' power:

> "Therefore, in order to keep me from becoming conceited, I was given a thorn in my flesh, a messenger of Satan, to torment me. Three times I pleaded with the Lord to take it away from me. But he said to me, 'My grace is sufficient for you, for my power is made perfect in weakness.' Therefore I will boast all the more gladly about my weaknesses, so that Christ's power may rest on me. That is why, for Christ's sake, I delight in weaknesses, in insults, in hardships, in persecutions, in difficulties. For when I am weak, then I am strong."
>
> (2 Corinthians 12 v 7-10)

Paul had an impeccable Jewish heritage and an intimate relationship with God. He was clever and courageous. He had a lot to be conceited about! But Jesus taught him that his power is made perfect in weakness, not in strength. So Paul delighted in attempting things he was naturally not good at, and in carrying on when he was opposed or encountered difficulties, because he knew that those things were necessary conditions for seeing Jesus' power at work.

This is what we need to remember when our confidence takes a knock. When we try something and it goes wrong, or when we are criticised or belittled for our contribution, the temptation is to give up. Instead, we can see this as a God-given opportunity. He is showing us our weakness so that we can put our confidence in him rather than in ourselves.

Think about a way that you or your church could serve Jesus that feels too difficult to try. Your weakness is never a reason not to try hard things for Jesus; it's a reason to expect his strength to work in you. Strong opposition isn't a reason to give up; it's a reason to expect Jesus' power to rest on you. Difficulties you face aren't reasons to think again; they're reasons to rely on Jesus' strength instead of your own.

Strength through the wimpy

Have you noticed that when Hollywood portrays biblical characters, they're played by muscle-bound actors? Russell Crowe as Noah, Christian Bale as Moses... I fear that one day they'll make a film about Gideon starring Jason Statham.

Because in reality, Gideon was a wimp. He was one of the judges, those who were raised up by God to rule the tribes of Israel before they had a king. When we first meet Gideon, he's threshing grain in a winepress, because he's scared of the Midianites who are occupying the land. Threshing needs wind, and a winepress is a big pit, so this is a coward's plan—it's like trying to fly a kite in a nuclear bunker.

But God chooses to do great things through Gideon precisely because he's such a wimp. God uses weak people so that no one is in any doubt that the strength comes from God. Judges 6 – 8 is a diary of a wimpy kid, and it's designed to press home this point:

- Gideon's pedigree is weak: he's the wimpiest kid in the wimpiest clan in Manasseh, but he will be able to strike down the armies of Midian because the strong LORD will be with him (Judges 6 v 11-24).

- Gideon's courage is weak: he's told by God to tear down Baal's altar but he does it at night because he's scared. Then he hides behind the curtains and lets his dad defend him when the angry locals come calling in the morning (v 25-32).
- Gideon's faith is weak: even though God has promised to be with him, he demands two signs that God will really do what he's said. He rolls out a fleece and asks God to soak the fleece but not the ground, and then the ground but not the fleece. Yet God's patience is strong with this wet blanket (Gideon, not the fleece), and he provides the signs (v 33-40).
- Gideon's army is weak: even though he's facing 135,000 Midianites, God whittles his army down from 32,000 soldiers to just 300. With odds of 450 to 1 against, they won't be able to boast that they won the battle by their own strength (7 v 1-8).
- Gideon's resolve is weak: he's afraid to attack the Midianites. But God's kindness is strong, so he arranges for Gideon to hear one Midianite soldier tell another about a dream he had in which Gideon destroys their camp. That way Gideon can know that they're more afraid of him than he is of them (v 9-16).
- Gideon's resources are weak: his 300 soldiers are armed with just trumpets, torches and empty tankards. But God is strong, and he creates such panic in the enemy camp that the Midianites turn on each other and then flee for the border (v 17-25).

God works through weakness so that no one will boast, "My own strength has saved me" (7 v 2). Human weakness isn't a barrier to God's strength; it's the channel for it. The bigger the task and the smaller you feel, the more it will force you to rely on God, and the more likely he is to work in you and through you. Lots of non-Christians are able to do lots of good, hard, courageous acts when they feel strong; Christians can also do them when we feel weak.

Remember this when you hear yourself making those excuses. Your weakness is paired with Jesus' strength.

I can't... but God can.

I'd never be able to... but Jesus is able to.

I don't feel like the right person... but these weaknesses make me exactly the right person for the Lord's strength to work in.

It's impossible for me... but nothing is impossible with God.

Strength in the weary

Following Jesus is hard. We meet lots of setbacks, and it's easy to become discouraged. We feel weary—at times, almost burned out. It feels impossible to carry on to the end. The thought of giving up and taking it easy is really appealing. Like that of a marathon runner hitting the wall, our run becomes a walk, then a shuffle, then a crawl, and then a collapse.

The promises of Isaiah 40 are made to people like us:

"Do you not know?
   Have you not heard?
The LORD is the everlasting God,
   the Creator of the ends of the earth.
He will not grow tired or weary,
   and his understanding no one can fathom.
He gives strength to the weary
   and increases the power of the weak.
Even youths grow tired and weary,

and young men stumble and fall;
    but those who hope in the LORD
        will renew their strength.
    They will soar on wings like eagles;
        they will run and not grow weary,
        they will walk and not be faint." (Isaiah 40 v 28-31)

God never grows weary. His strength never runs out. Therefore the supply of his strength to us will never run out either. We have limits to our energy and motivation and sanity, but God's resources are limitless. When we put our hope in his strength rather than ours, we are energised. Instead of crawling or collapsing, we can soar on wings like eagles (even without a Red Bull).

So there is no need to fear that we won't be able to finish something that God calls us to start. This is not a reason never to rest and proudly think we need never sleep. But it is a reason to trust in God's strength. When our resources come to an end, we'll be forced to rely on God's resources, which never end.

No strength for the waverer

When we're weak, wimpy or weary, we will find God's strength flowing through us as we rely on him. But when we waver, we will not. Asa was king of Judah. In his youth, he boldly relied on the Lord and served him. When huge armies from Cush and Libya invaded he prayed to the Lord and bravely led his armies into battle, and the Lord gave him a great victory to protect his people from the oppressive empire.

But when Asa reached middle age, he wavered. When a neighbouring king threatened him, he didn't pray for the Lord's help, but instead took the treasures of the Lord's temple and sent them to the king of Aram to buy his help. I guess lots of us become risk-averse in middle age, and more "prudent" in how we serve and make sacrifices for Jesus. With a house, a job, a pension, a mortgage, a spouse, a family, or a reputation, we become more conscious of what we've got to lose. But this is what God said to Asa through one of his prophets:

> "At that time Hanani the seer came to Asa king of Judah and said to him: 'Because you relied on the king of Aram and not on the LORD your God, the army of the king of Aram has escaped from your hand. Were not the Cushites and Libyans a mighty army with great numbers of chariots and horsemen? Yet when you relied on the LORD, he delivered them into your hand. *For the eyes of the LORD range throughout the earth to strengthen those whose hearts are fully committed to him.* You have done a foolish thing, and from now on you will be at war.'" (2 Chronicles 16 v 7-9, my italics)

God loves to strengthen his people to serve him and do good in the world, so he has his binoculars out to scan for anyone who needs his strength. What sort of person is he looking for? "Those whose hearts are fully committed to him"—people with undivided hearts; people who don't waver in the face of difficulty, but who are willing to live with the discomfort of relying totally on the Lord they can't see. You won't miss out on the Lord's strength through being too feeble, but you might by being too safe. Jesus strengthens the weak, the wimpy and the weary—but not the wavering.

How the Lord strengthens us
Timothy was a young church leader who had learned his trade beside the apostle Paul. Now he had been given responsibility

for some churches in Ephesus, while Paul languished in prison. Timothy faced a daunting task. He was on his own, there were popular false teachers in the churches, and he faced the possibility of his own arrest. He was young, inexperienced, and a natural coward. How could he ever fulfil the responsibility that Jesus had entrusted to him?

Paul wrote to him:

> "For this reason I remind you to fan into flame the gift of God, which is in you through the laying on of my hands. For the Spirit God gave us does not make us timid, but gives us power, love and self-discipline. So do not be ashamed of the testimony about our Lord or of me his prisoner. Rather, join with me in suffering for the gospel, by the power of God." (2 Timothy 1 v 6-8)

God has given you the same Spirit that he gave Timothy. If you trust Jesus, then Jesus' Spirit is now your Spirit. Jesus strengthens you by giving you a Spirit of power, love and self-discipline. That makes all the difference.

If you are a Christian, the Spirit who lives in you is the same Spirit by whom God made the galaxies (Psalm 33 v 6). The Spirit who lives in you is the same Spirit who lived in Jesus and strengthened him in his earthly ministry (Acts 10 v 37-38). The Spirit who lives in you is the same Spirit through whom God raised Jesus from the dead (Romans 8 v 9-11). He is the Spirit of power.

The Spirit of power works in all Jesus' followers. He has made you into a new person, and is giving you new desires to love God and those around you. So don't believe the lie that you can never change. Don't live as though you will always be the cowardly escapist you once were and sometimes (if you're anything like me) still are. Don't assume that because you gave up last time, you will give up next time. The Spirit of power is in you. He can keep you going when you're on your own, when you face opposition, and when you suffer for your faith.

The Spirit of power also works through all Jesus' followers. When you think that something won't work, or won't make any difference, this is what you need to remember. Jesus doesn't call you to serve him because he needs your contribution. He calls you to serve him because he wants you to share in the joyful privilege of being part of his mission. So he isn't limited by your limitations. He knows them and will turn them to his advantage in his plan.

My experience of following Jesus is that I go around trying to serve Jesus and screwing up pretty much everything. Later I might discover that it helped someone, and I'm left asking, "How on earth did that happen?" Answer: the Spirit of power worked through me.

The next characteristic of the Spirit that Paul mentioned to Timothy is more surprising. We can see how having the Spirit of power cures cowardice, but why mention the Spirit of "love"? It's because when we are afraid, we are thinking about ourselves. "How can I do this?" "What if I fail?" "It's too hard for me." We do what is easiest for us, rather than what is best for others, because we are focused on ourselves.

This is what the 20th-century Welsh preacher Martyn Lloyd-Jones said in his classic treatment of this verse:

> "There is only one way to get rid of self, and that is that you should become so absorbed in someone or something else that you have no time to think about yourself. Thank God, the Spirit of God makes that possible. He is not only 'the spirit of power', but he is also 'the spirit of love'." (*Spiritual Depression*, page 103)

The only way to stop being self-centred and self-absorbed is to be self-forgetful. The only way to stop caring so much about me is to start caring more about others. This is what the Spirit of love does in us. He pours out God's love into our hearts (Romans 5 v 5-8). When we know that Jesus lives for us, we are freed from needing to live for ourselves any more. We focus on other people's needs and not on our own. Our hearts beat to the rhythm of love, not fear.

My young children love the Octonauts. The Octonauts are eight cartoon animals who help underwater creatures. Peso the Penguin is their medic, and he is often a trembling coward. He's afraid of anything big, or dark, or unknown. In one episode, his friends are trapped inside a whale shark; and he's too scared to try and help them. But Peso, while a coward, is also very loving. When he realises the whale shark is in pain, his compassion takes over. He forgets about himself, and is only concerned for the shark. He courageously approaches the shark to treat it, and in doing so is able to rescue his friends. Love conquers fear.

The same is true for us (although, since we aren't cartoon characters, this kind of self-forgetting love doesn't come naturally to our hearts). So ask the Spirit of love to conquer your fears. Reflect each day on God's love for you. Plead for the Spirit to help you to see the orphaned, the bereaved, the exploited, the lonely and the lost as he sees them. Pray that you would forget about your weaknesses and needs, and instead be concerned for others in their weakness and need. You can become strong and courageous because God has given you the Spirit of love.

Lastly, the Spirit at work in you is the Spirit of "self-discipline". Good intentions aren't enough on their own. I may want to do more exercise, read my Bible each day and spend less time on social media, but I won't be able to without self-discipline. My past might be a litany of failed New Year's resolutions and short-lived interests, but that doesn't mean my future has to be. I may never have completed a diet, a Bible-reading programme, an exercise plan or a DIY project in the past, but with the Spirit's strength, in the future I can. The Spirit doesn't just change our hearts; he can also change our habits. He can give us the resolve and the self-control to put our good intentions into practice.

So when you need to reduce your dependence on alcohol or chocolate, ask the Spirit to give you self-discipline. When you want to make a weekly commitment to serve at church but worry that you'll let people down again, trust the Spirit for strength to keep it up. When you want to cut back on your time playing computer games or watching daytime TV so you can serve the people around you, pray that the Spirit would give you self-control with the remote control. Whenever God calls you to a task that is too hard for you alone, remember that he has given you the Spirit of self-discipline to help you. You have the Spirit; and so you have every reason to be able to change, and no excuse not to.

The Lord is my strength

Popeye has spinach. Superman's powers come from the sun. Your strength comes from the Lord. Your weakness is never a reason to hold back from a challenge, because it is in your weakness that God's strength is made perfect. Like Wilberforce, when you are weak you will know both "your need for help, and where to look for it", as Newton wrote all those years ago.

In 1793, when Wilberforce was fighting against the slave trade, another William arrived in India. William Carey was a pioneer missionary and evangelist often known as the "father of modern missions". He also published the first books on the botany of India, introduced the steam engine and the printing press, campaigned for the rights of women and lepers, introduced a savings bank, started the first newspaper in an oriental language, founded dozens of schools and pioneered lending libraries. That is some list! How much of that would have seemed possible to him before he set off? But Carey knew that God's strength works through our weakness. This was his motto:

"Attempt great things for God;
expect great things from God."

Pause and reflect on whether there is any impossible-looking task that God is calling you or your church to attempt. It might be a radical lifestyle change. It might be challenging a massive injustice in the world. It might be starting a new ministry or planting a new church or going abroad as a missionary. The size of the challenge and the weakness that you feel aren't obstacles to God's strength—they're the channels for it, because they will force you to be relying on him.

"Attempt great things for God;
expect great things from God."

What good, bold or difficult thing are you considering not doing today because you can't do it? The Lord is your strength. Go do it.

MY STRENGTH

MY SHEPHERD

MY REFUGE

MY ROCK

Jesus is...

MY PORTION

MY LIGHT

10. Salvation

"The LORD is ... my salvation."

Psalm 27 v 1

It should have been the best day of his life. Instead, it sent him to prison.

On 26th April 2013, Neil McArdle was due to marry his fiancée, Amy Williams, at Liverpool's magnificent St George's Hall. But the night before, he discovered that he had failed to fill in the form to book the venue.

He should have told his fiancée his mistake. But he was afraid of letting her down, afraid of looking stupid, and afraid of saying sorry. So he did what any other panicking escapist would do—on the morning of the ceremony he went to a phone box, rang the venue, and said in a disguised voice:

"This is not a hoax call. There's a bomb in St George's Hall and it will go off in 45 minutes."

The disguise in his voice was not enough to avoid detection. Neil was given 12 months in jail for his stupidity (though at the time of sentencing, Amy was still sticking with him). He thought his lie would cover his tracks and save him from embarrassment, but instead it catapulted his story into the national media.

It's not too hard to detect the damage caused in our lives when we are trapped by similar fears—the blame we put on others when we're afraid of looking stupid, the lies we tell when we're afraid of saying sorry, and the risks we don't take because we're afraid of failure. We long to be transformed from fearful to fearless. And once again the key is to look at Jesus. As the evangelist Glen Scrivener puts it:

> "Fear is when life overwhelms us. Faith is when Christ overwhelms us." (http://bit.ly/2tFPkv1)

So here is one final picture to help you stand in awe of the Lord Jesus with an undivided heart. The Lord is your salvation. This picture tells you that whatever else happens (or might happen), you have been saved from your greatest enemy. Your deepest fear will never be realised. With that knowledge, you can be transformed from fearful to fearless.

Fearful

Most of us know the story of David and Goliath; few of us understand who we are in the story. We read about the plucky young underdog felling the evil giant, and assume that we're meant to be like David, the courageous hero. But that's not good news—because when we meet our "Goliaths", we don't tend to be very courageous or heroic.

The good news is that God doesn't want us to identify with David. He wants us to identify with the other Israelites: with the soldiers who were too scared to fight, who were saved by David, and who were transformed from fearful to fearless. Let's see how that happens as we collapse on the sofa to watch this episode from the 1 Samuel box set...

On one side of the valley of Elah stood the army of the Philistines. On the other side quivered the army of Israel. Every day for 40 days, Goliath came out of the Philistine ranks and bellowed the same challenge:

"Choose a man and let him come down to me. If he is able to fight and kill me, we will become your subjects; but if I overcome him and kill him, you will become our subjects and serve us ... This day I defy the armies of Israel! Give me a man and let us fight each other."

(1 Samuel 17 v 8-10)

Be afraid, yelled Goliath. *Be very afraid...* And they were— every day for 40 days the knees in the Israelite ranks knocked with the same dread:

"On hearing the Philistine's words, Saul and all the Israelites were dismayed and terrified ... Whenever the Israelites saw the man, they all fled from him in great fear." (v 11, 24)

Fear led to flight. They escaped.

And don't we know that feeling?! We keep our aspirations low to save ourselves from the possibility of failure. We avoid people or make excuses to save us from the humiliation of saying sorry. We step back from messy relationships to save us from a situation we can't control and make perfect. Instead of rising to the challenge, we run from it. Instead of standing strong and courageous, we cower and hide. Instead of being fearless, we are fearful.

Fearsome

Goliath was certainly fearsome. Here is the Bible's description of this human tank:

"His height was six cubits and a span [nine feet]. He had a bronze helmet on his head and wore a coat of scale armour of bronze weighing five thousand shekels [58 kg]; on his legs he wore bronze greaves, and a bronze javelin was slung on his back. His spear shaft was like a weaver's rod, and its iron point weighed six hundred shekels [6.9 kg/15 pounds]. His shield-bearer went ahead of him." (1 Samuel 17 v 4-7)

The Israelites had good reason to fear. First up, they faced a fearsome enemy. The Philistines had fought and oppressed Israel for generations. And Goliath was "The Philistine"— the undefeated champion of the ancient world. Who could possibly go into the ring with him and survive? And so they also faced a fearsome slavery. Defeat to Goliath— and that defeat was inevitable—meant becoming the Philistines' subjects and serving them as slaves (1 Samuel 17 v 9). Israelite women and children, cities and crops would all belong to the occupying forces. There was only one alternative option—to face a fearsome death. Goliath's size, his armour, his spear, his javelin, his shield and his undefeated record as a champion all meant certain death for anyone who confronted him.

We also have good reasons to be afraid. We face a fearsome enemy. As Goliath sought to devour Israel, so Satan seeks to devour God's people today (1 Peter 5 v 8). As he deceives us with his sweet little lies (Genesis 3 v 4-5; John 8 v 44), we face a fearsome slavery. "Everyone who sins is a slave to sin," said Jesus (John 8 v 34). Sin is more addictive than crack. It captivates us with promises it never quite keeps. So however hard we try to do what is best, we keep doing what is easiest. However many resolutions we make, we never achieve integrity. However many times we tell ourselves to take more risks, we can't kick the habit of playing safe. We may be free to do what we want, but we're powerless to want what is good. And this means that we face a fearsome death. Death is going to break all our relationships and undo all our achievements. Our looks, our intelligence, our talents and our virtues will rot in the grave or be consumed in the crematorium. Nothing that we own will be ours any longer. The chances of any of our own great-grandchildren knowing our name are humiliatingly low. We're all going to die, and our reluctance to think about that fact shows how afraid we are of it.

Satan, slavery and death. They are our greatest enemies. They are, or should be, our deepest fears. All we can do as we think about them is quake—which is why we so often aim to ignore them.

In the face of such fearsome foes, how can we ever become fearless?

Fearless

In the valley of Elah, just one man was fearless. In the previous chapter, young David had been anointed as king of God's people, and God's Spirit had come upon him in power (1 Samuel 16 v 13). When David heard Goliath's challenge, he responded with courage:

> "Let no one lose heart on account of this Philistine;
> your servant will go and fight him ... Your servant has
> killed both the lion and the bear; this uncircumcised
> Philistine will be like one of them, because he has
> defied the armies of the living God. The Lord who
> rescued me from the paw of the lion and the paw of the
> bear will rescue me from the hand of this Philistine."
>
> (17 v 32, 36-37)

David may have had confidence in God, but nobody else had confidence in him. His older brother Eliab rebuked him for being proud and leaving his chores undone. King Saul told him he couldn't win because he was too young and inexperienced. Goliath himself mocked David for his weakness and his inadequate weapons.

But David knew that he came in the name of the LORD, and so the LORD would save his people through him:

> "All those gathered here will know that it is not by
> sword or spear that the LORD saves; for the battle is the
> LORD's, and he will give all of you into our hands."
>
> (1 Samuel 17 v 47)

As expected, the battle was over before it had barely begun. What was unexpected was the result. One stone, one sling, one shot to the head, and *Goliath* lay lifeless on the ground. David the fearless king had won a great salvation for his people. And his people knew it. They were utterly transformed:

> "When the Philistines saw that their hero was dead,
> they turned and ran. Then the men of Israel and
> Judah surged forward with a shout and pursued the
> Philistines to the entrance of Gath and to the gates of
> Ekron." (1 Samuel 17 v 51-52)

Instead of stepping backward or freezing in fear, the Israelites now surged forward to take on the enemy. There was no enemy to be scared of any longer, no slavery to worry about, no death to fear. Their greatest enemies were helpless. Their deepest fears weren't going to happen. Their king had won the victory for them, and now they could enjoy the spoils.

David is a shadow showing us the outline of our real fearless hero. At his baptism, Jesus was anointed as King of God's people, and God's Spirit rested on him. He faced criticism, opposition, bloodthirsty crowds and demonic powers without flinching. He entered Jerusalem in the name of the Lord, confident that his Father would save his people through him.

Nobody else had confidence in him. His closest friend, Peter, rebuked him for saying he would suffer and die. His other followers deserted him and fled. The Romans mocked his claim to be a king, and the Jewish leaders taunted him for not even being able to save himself.

But on the cross, Jesus faced Satan, sin and death. He fought the decisive battle against our worst enemies, and he won:

> "Since the children have flesh and blood, [Jesus] too shared in their humanity so that by his death he might break the power of him who holds the power of death—that is, the devil—and free those who all their lives were held in slavery by their fear of death."
>
> (Hebrews 2 v 14-15)

By taking our punishment, Jesus broke Satan's power. By bearing our sins, Jesus freed us from slavery. By dying the death we should have died, Jesus has removed any reason to fear death. Jesus the fearless King has won a great salvation for his people.

When our hearts grasp this reality, we are made new. Like the Israelite soldiers, we are transformed from fearful to fearless. Instead of stepping backward or freezing in fear, we now surge forward. There is no need to be scared of Satan any longer, there is no slavery to worry about, no death to fear. Our greatest enemies are helpless. The worst that could happen to us won't happen. Those things we should fear the most we need not fear at all. Our King has won the victory for us, and now we can enjoy the spoils.

Enjoying the spoils

Here are three real-life pictures of what it looks like to enjoy the spoils of the King's victory.

First, we have a preacher in the 9th century BC. Jonah is probably the Bible's most infamous escapist. But he discovered the wonderful truth that God is the God of second chances.

The first time that God called him to preach his message of repentance in Nineveh, "Jonah ran away from the LORD" (Jonah 1 v 1-3). Instead of going east across the land to Nineveh, he headed west across the sea to Tarshish. He fancied the sandy beaches of Spain more than the sandy deserts of Iraq. He did what looked easiest for himself, rather than what was best for the pagan enemies that God was concerned for.

One storm, one near-death experience and one strange vomiting fish later, God called Jonah to preach in Nineveh again. And this time Jonah obeyed. He went to the intimidating capital city of a violent pagan empire and spoke God's message (3 v 1-4).

What made the difference in Jonah? His poem of grateful praise in chapter 2 shows that he had discovered that the Lord was his salvation.

"To the roots of the mountains I sank down;
    the earth barred me in for ever.
But you, LORD my God,
    brought my life up from the pit.
When my life was ebbing away,
    I remembered you, LORD,
and my prayer rose to you,
    to your holy temple.
Those who cling to worthless idols
    turn away from God's love for them.

But I, with shouts of grateful praise,
   will sacrifice to you.
What I have vowed I will make good.
   I will say, 'Salvation comes from the LORD.'"

(Jonah 2 v 6-9)

The Lord had rescued Jonah from his own sinful stupidity, from certain death, and from divine judgment. The worst that could have happened to Jonah hadn't happened. This experience of salvation gave Jonah courage to obey. Even if he was laughed at in Nineveh, his sin was forgiven. Even if he was beaten up, he had been rescued from death. Chapter 4 suggests that Jonah had much more to learn about God's grace, but the courage he did show came from knowing that the Lord was his salvation.

Second, let me introduce you to a teenager in the 1st century BC. She was called Mary. In Christmas nativity plays, every parent wants their daughter to be Mary. She's the star of the show—she meets the angel, she rides the donkey, she gives birth to the Messiah. But the reality was darker. Mary was an unmarried teenager in a very traditional Middle-Eastern society.

Here's what she knew as she listened to the angel. Gabriel was asking her to bear the shame of getting pregnant before her wedding day. She was being invited to risk her relationship with Joseph, who would want to divorce her when he found out. She was being told to give up whatever other hopes and dreams she had for her life.

Here's what she didn't know, but would find out. She would endure a long journey while nine months pregnant. She would face the dangers of giving birth in a dirty animal shelter. She would flee her native land as a refugee because her king wanted to kill her son. And years later, and worst of all, she would watch her firstborn son be tortured to death on a Roman cross.

And Mary answered:

> "I am the Lord's servant ... May your word to me be
> fulfilled." (Luke 1 v 38)

Not even, *I'll do it if I have to.* But, *I'll do it because I want to.* The fact that Mary welcomed the angel's news was almost as great a miracle as the fact that a virgin would have a child. What gave Mary the courage to accept all this uncertainty and shame? She knew that the Lord was her salvation:

> "My soul glorifies the Lord
>   and my spirit rejoices in God my Saviour,
> for he has been mindful
>   of the humble state of his servant.
> From now on all generations will call me blessed,
>   for the Mighty One has done great things for me—
>   holy is his name." (Luke 1 v 46-49)

Mary understood that through her son, God was acting to save his people. The Mighty One was acting to put the world right. Her Saviour was about to defeat Satan and sin and death. If she could be saved from them, then her honour and safety and marriage and hopes were a price worth paying. The worst that could happen wouldn't happen. Rejoicing in God's salvation made obedience possible.

Thirdly, I want to take you to a reader of this book in the 21st century. To you. What difference will it make to you to know that Jesus has dealt with your greatest enemies and your deepest fears?

This picture will help you to confront your past failures. Perhaps you live in denial about a health problem or addiction because the truth is too painful. Or you tell lies and make excuses to cover up what you've done. Or you might have a tendency to blame others for your mistakes—your parents, your (lack of) education, the person who made you angry.

But Jesus has died for sinners, taking away the condemnation that Satan used to make us slaves. So sorry is no longer the hardest word. If a man tells the truth to his fiancée about messing up the booking and she leaves him, he still has eternal life. If a boss admits to her company that she's been covering up her team's losses and gets sacked, she has still been freed from Satan's power. A pastor can confess his wrongdoing to his congregation, a mum to her children, and a politician to their country, because whatever the consequences, they are forgiven by God.

Is there a mistake or a sin that you've been covering up? You can fearlessly take your share of the blame, and offer to make amends to anyone you have harmed, because Jesus is still your salvation.

This picture will also help you to confront future failures. Maybe you procrastinate because you are a perfectionist waiting for the perfect moment to confront a problem or complete a task. Or perhaps you micro-manage and hate entrusting others with responsibility because you're a bit of a control freak and worry they'll mess things up. Or maybe you would love to take the step of starting your own business, or inviting someone to church, or sharing a poem you've written, but the risk feels as if it's too much.

You will be free to take risks, free to let go and free to fail when you know deep in your being that the worst that could happen to you won't happen. You can start that awkward conversation now, because even if it doesn't go well, Jesus' kingdom will still come. You can delegate to people who aren't as talented or experienced as you, because even if they don't do things your way, you still share in Jesus' victory. You can have high aspirations that you might not reach, because even if you fail, you are still saved. As my ever-loving wife delights to remind me whenever she beats me in a game, "Don't worry—God loves failures!"

Is there something that you're holding back from trying because it feels too risky and you're afraid of failure? Remember that Jesus has defeated your greatest enemies and dealt with your deepest fears. Every morning you can wake up and know that whatever you do, God will be delighted with you when you go to bed because you are in Christ and share his righteousness. You can go forward and enjoy the spoils of his victory. The Lord is your salvation.

11. The hardest things we *do*

Reading a book on escaping escapism is the easy bit. Doing something about what you've read is the harder part.

I'm guessing the fact you're still reading means that these seven pictures have helped you to see Jesus in new ways. But how can that make a real difference and a lasting difference? How do you leave your escapist ways behind and start walking in the paths of commitment, courage and integrity?

This book has probably challenged you. As you look at your life, it may feel as if you have a mountain—or many mountains—to climb. But don't let that put you off; you can climb the metaphorical mountains that you face in the same way I climb physical mountains.

Here's how.

1. Choose your mountain
I would never try to climb all the mountains in the world (or even in Scotland) at once. They have to be tackled one at a time. And I don't set off with a vague idea of which peak I

might scale today. I read the books and study the maps and pick my next target.

You also need to choose your next mountain. Don't try to conquer all your escapism at once. Narrow it down. Focus on one growth area. And don't come away from this book with a vague idea that you'd like to be less fearful. Set a goal.

Pray. Ask the Spirit how he wants you to become more like Jesus. Which difficult person do you need to love? What difficult task do you need to tackle? What difficult situation do you need to persevere in? What is the next room in the house of your heart that Jesus wants to renovate? When do you need to be strong and courageous? Which challenge would you love to rise to?

Don't be vague ("I want to take more risks"). Make your goal as specific as possible ("I will speak to someone new at church each Sunday"). Visualise it. What does it look like, feel like, sound like, smell like? Some people find it helpful to make a picture of it. Don't make your goal a negative ("I want to be less tied to my phone"). State it positively ("I want to give the children my full attention"). Write it down.

Think big! Aim high! Start praying that God will give you an undivided heart that is able to climb this mountain.

2. Know your starting point

As well as knowing the destination, before I can plan my route up the mountain, I also need to know my starting point.

In what ways do you fall short of your goal at the moment? Ask the Spirit to show you how you are not like Christ in ways that result in you struggling. How do you fail to love difficult people, tackle difficult challenges and persevere in difficult times? What are your sins of omission? This needs self-awareness, and you might well find it helpful to ask the people who know you best to tell you. What matters is being honest. You need to know where you are before you can head towards that peak on the horizon.

Then dig deeper. Why are you like this? What are you scared of, or in awe of, when you escape? What fears have torn your heart?

Does this sin come from...

... fear of hard work?

... or fear of being hurt?

... or fear of other people?

... or fear of missing out?

... or fear of not being able to cope?

... or fear of letting people down?

... or fear of failure?

... or fear of something else?

Pray that you will be able to fight this fear with the fear of God.

3. Gather your companions

Some mountaineers do climb solo—but they are the exception. The best mountain days are shared with friends. They keep you going when the path is steep and the wind is in your face. They enjoy the view with you at the summit.

No one can follow Jesus solo. No one becomes like him on their own. The more ambitious your goal, the more setbacks you will face and struggles you will have to negotiate. So you need to find some Christian friends, or a pastor, or a small-group leader, or someone you live with, who will walk with you. They will help you to set your goal, and remind you of it if ever you're tempted to stand still or turn around. They will pray for you and with you. They will encourage you with the progress you've already made. They will celebrate with you at the summit.

Pray about who to ask. Then tell them the mountain you have chosen and ask them to walk with you.

4. Plan your route

Work out how to get from where you are to where you want to be. Break the journey down. How is your goal going to become reality? What action steps do you need to take? There might be a conversation you need to have, or a habit you need to start. One of your steps might be something you need to give up, or give away. As one of my steps, I've just made an appointment with the dentist. Be practical. Be specific. Keep praying.

5. Pack your bags

Don't set out on the hills empty-handed. You need to carry food that will keep you going. That food is the pictures of Jesus we've been looking at in this book. They are what will change your heart and guide your steps. Is there a particular picture to focus on?

- When you're afraid of hard work, the Lord is your refuge.
- When you're afraid of being hurt, the Lord is your shepherd.
- When you're afraid of what people think, the Lord is your light.
- When you're afraid of missing out, the Lord is your portion.
- When you're afraid of not being able to cope in the storm, the Lord is your Rock.
- When you're afraid of letting people down, the Lord is your strength.

- When you're afraid of failure, the Lord is your salvation.

God put these images in the Bible to stir our imagination. Visualising Jesus in these ways helps move these truths from our heads to our hearts. So re-read the chapter, or chapters, that point to the pictures of Jesus that you most need. Memorise a Bible verse that describes the Lord in that way. Pray the picture into your heart. Actually imagine yourself as a soldier in a castle, or a sheep following a shepherd to the green pastures. Put a picture of the sun or a delicious meal as the home screen on your phone to remind yourself that Jesus is your light or your portion. Play the video in your mind of you, clinging to a rock in a storm. When the crunch comes, be ready to say to yourself, "The Lord is my..."

6. Start your journey
The road to nowhere is paved with great plans and careful preparations. A mountain isn't climbed until you lace up your boots, get out of the door, start walking, and keep walking.

You need to start. The only way to become courageous is to start doing courageous things. Don't put it off any longer. Picture Jesus, pray, and take that first step!

7. Celebrate your progress
When I'm back from a day in the mountains, safe and warm, it's time to look back at the day with a drink in my hand. Some days I look back and celebrate a mountain climbed. Other days I got lost or tired or wet or cold, and I didn't make it to the top.

So in a few weeks or months, take time to look back and see how far you've come. Set a date now when you'll sit down and evaluate your progress. If you've reached your goal, praise

God! Be encouraged at how he's worked in your life, thank him with your companions, and choose your next mountain.

If you haven't reached your goal yet, pray to God! Ask him for help to persevere. Work out what you need to adjust for the future. Are there steps you've missed out? Is there another picture of Jesus that will calm your fears?

You have a mountain to climb—and that is intimidating. The weather may be closing in. Your legs may feel like lead. But it's worth aiming high. It's worth keeping going. It's worth struggling on.

It's worth loving difficult people. It's worth tackling difficult tasks. It's worth persevering in difficult times.

Because the hardest things we do are usually also the best.

Thank you...

I owe "thank yous" to more people than I can mention here, but especially I owe them...

... to Helen, my wife, for putting up with me and encouraging me to get this off my chest.

... to my children, Ben, Rhodri, Sophie and Abi, for being well worth turning my phone off for.

... to the people at St Cleopas and St Gabriel's, Toxteth, where I was serving when I wrote this—for loving us, letting me make mistakes, and helping me to learn lots during the brilliant four years we were with you.

... to Carl Laferton, my editor, for all your skills in improving the raw material you were working with.

... to Matt and Paul, for keeping me on the rails through your friendship, prayer and admonishment.

... and most of all to the Lord Jesus—my refuge, my shepherd, my light, my portion, my rock, my strength, my salvation and my God—for everything.

thegoodbook
COMPANY

BIBLICAL | RELEVANT | ACCESSIBLE

At The Good Book Company, we are dedicated to helping Christians and local churches grow. We believe that God's growth process always starts with hearing clearly what he has said to us through his timeless word—the Bible.

Ever since we opened our doors in 1991, we have been striving to produce resources that honour God in the way the Bible is used. We have grown to become an international provider of user-friendly resources to the Christian community, with believers of all backgrounds and denominations using our Bible studies, books, evangelistic resources, DVD-based courses and training events.

We want to equip ordinary Christians to live for Christ day by day, and churches to grow in their knowledge of God, their love for one another, and the effectiveness of their outreach.

Call us for a discussion of your needs or visit one of our local websites for more information on the resources and services we provide.

Your friends at The Good Book Company

UK & EUROPE		thegoodbook.co.uk	0333 123 0880
NORTH AMERICA		thegoodbook.com	866 244 2165
AUSTRALIA		thegoodbook.com.au	(02) 9564 3555
NEW ZEALAND		thegoodbook.co.nz	(+64) 3 343 2463

 WWW.CHRISTIANITYEXPLORED.ORG
Our partner site is a great place for those exploring the Christian faith, with a clear explanation of the good news, powerful testimonies and answers to difficult questions.